# EMILY DICKINSON

*In the same series*

The Plays of Samuel Beckett
Selected Poems of Ezra Pound
Selected Poems of T. S. Eliot
Seamus Heaney
Edward Thomas

Faber Student Guides

# EMILY DICKINSON
## Looking to Canaan

## John Robinson

*faber and faber*
LONDON · BOSTON

First published in 1986 by
Faber and Faber Limited
3 Queen Square London WC1N 3AU

Printed in Great Britain by
Redwood Burn Ltd Trowbridge Wiltshire

© John Robinson 1986

*British Library Cataloguing in Publication Data*

Robinson, John, *1943–*
Emily Dickinson – Looking to Canaan: students' guide.
1. Dickinson, Emily — Criticism and interpretation.
I.    Title
811' .4          PS1541.Z5

ISBN 0-571-13943-4

*Library of Congress Cataloging-in-Publication Data*

Robinson, John.
Emily Dickinson.
(A Faber student guide)
Bibliography: p.
1. Dickinson, Emily, 1830–1886—Criticism and interpretation.
I. Title.    II. Series.
PS1541.R63    1986      811'.4      86-11605
ISBN 0-571-13943-4 (pbk.)

To my mother

# The Faber Student Guides

In an age when critical theory promises, or threatens, to 'cross over' into literature and to become its own object of study, there is a powerful case for re-asserting the primacy of the literary text. The Faber Student Guides are intended in the first instance to provide substantial critical introductions to writers of major importance. Although each contributor inevitably writes from a considered critical position, it is not the aim of the series to impose a uniformity of theoretical approach. Each Guide will make use of biographical material and each will conclude with a select bibliography which will in all cases take note of the latest developments usefully relevant to the subject. Beyond that, however, contributors have been chosen for their critical abilities as well as for their familiarity with the subject of their choice.

Although the primary aim of the series is to focus attention on individual writers, there will be exceptions. Among our future plans are studies of the fiction of the First and Second World Wars; and of Edwardian drama. And although the majority of writers or periods studied will be of the twentieth century, this is not intended to preclude other writers or periods – as the study of Emily Dickinson shows. Above all, the series aims to return readers to a sharpened awareness of those texts without which there would be no criticism.

John Lucas

Ah, but a man's reach should exceed his grasp,
Or what's a heaven for?

– Robert Browning, 'Andrea del Sarto'

# Contents

|       | Acknowledgements       | 8   |
|-------|------------------------|-----|
|       | Note on Usage          | 9   |
| I     | History and Her History| 11  |
| II    | Theatre of the World   | 34  |
| III   | Faulting God           | 69  |
| IV    | Nicodemus' Mystery     | 86  |
| V     | Of Some Strange Race   | 110 |
| VI    | Upon Enchanted Ground  | 137 |
|       | Notes                  | 178 |
|       | Bibliography           | 181 |
|       | Index                  | 183 |

# Acknowledgements

To Faber and Faber for permission to quote from *The Complete Poems of Emily Dickinson*, from T. S. Eliot's *Four Quartets* and from his *Selected Essays*; to The Belknap Press of Harvard University Press for material from *The Letters of Emily Dickinson* and from *The Poems of Emily Dickinson*; and to Eyre Methuen for permission to quote from 'Survivors' in Alan Ross's *Poems 1942–67*.

# Note on Usage

References to Emily Dickinson's poems (e.g. # 198) are to numbers and texts in the single-volume *Complete Poems* edited by Thomas H. Johnson, but checked against his three-volume variorum edition which I refer to as *Poems*. Poems which are identified by first line only and not by number will be found in the slim volume of poems selected by Ted Hughes. References to the letters (e.g. L 234) are to the numbers and texts in the standard three-volume edition, details of which are also to be found in the Bibliography.

# I

# History and Her History

People tell me that the *myth* will hear every note – she will be near, but unseen . . . Isn't that like a book? So interesting.

No one knows the cause of her isolation, but of course there are dozens of reasons assigned.[1]

'Tell it slant,' Emily Dickinson once advised ( # 1129). I want to begin, not with the nineteenth-century Amherst, Massachusetts, where she was born, but – though still in New England – some miles and years away in seventeenth-century Salem.

Notoriously, in 1692 her Puritan forebears were hanging witches there. Curious to know the future, young girls had made means to find out, amongst other things, about their likely marriages. The signs that they saw in the process frightened them and, in turn, their own disturbed behaviour alarmed their families who quickly regarded them as victims. Accusations were made. Trials were held. Enemies were executed.

But there were still more accusations, more trials, more executions, till the judicial process itself seemed to be out of control. Piercing glances, touches, tetchiness might be interpreted as the public signs of private connection with malign power – and the interpretation might be lethal. There was judgement in the eye of the beholder and, however reluctant they might be to convict on 'spectral testimony', the tendency of the courts was to make the insubstantial real. Fear and mistrust produced their own map of what, in reflections published the following year, the Reverend Cotton Mather called *The Wonders of the Invisible World.*

History was being made out of belief; and those crucial, investigative questions, why *now*? why *here*?, were not allowed their proper weight. History was accounted for in terms which left time and place out of the reckoning. There was an incompleteness in the human response, a failure of intelligence which was scarcely distinguishable from a failure of that confidence which we call love.

It is hardly likely that Emily Dickinson would have been guilty of such failure. So lightly ironic was she about received opinion, so independent of the rigidities of dogma, that it is difficult to see her being possessed by the destructive vigour of the judges of Salem. She was not so narrowly purposeful, yet her inheritance was that tradition which celebrated the timeless wonders of the invisible world, and, in manifold ways, she, too, tended to lock history out of her imagination. An obvious example is that, although there are soldiers, battlefields, and martial imagery in her poems, the American Civil War, which came in the middle of her life, is missing from them. More generally, many of her poems resist the reader's enquiries about the where and when of location, and so resist, too, the attendant why here? and why now? which are part of the attempt to form a judgement. She does not help us to see how she might have changed or developed as a poet. Her poems are often reluctant to locate us in the circumstances of their generation.

Salem in 1692 can help us to clarify this. The map of the invisible world which produced the witch trials was one which charted division and marked out us and them. Before the accusations began, a Salem Village faction in which the Putnam family was prominent felt itself to be on the defensive against newcomers from Salem Town. The Putnams named the Proctors and the Porters and thus, in the account of the historians Paul Boyer and Stephen Nissenbaum, deployed the power which divines such as Cotton Mather helped sustain to make history out of belief:

> The social order was being profoundly shaken by a superhuman force which had lured all too many into active complicity with it. We have chosen to construe this force as emergent mercantile capitalism. Mather, and Salem Village, called it witchcraft.[2]

From this rivalry of names we can see how much the flow of history is determined by interpreters. Those who sat in 1692 in the Court of Oyer and Terminer and decided that 'witch' was an appropriate and fatal name for Rebecca Nurse were as much interpreters as those who study them in the twentieth century. History not only can be patterned but has to be since we make the present out of expectations of the future and we ground those expectations in comparisons with the past.

We can also see that today we are still dealing with the invisible world and with its interpreters. The Empire of Evil has recently been relocated[3] and its site shifted elsewhere than the woods outside Salem, but we are involved not the less for that with matters of belief and authentication. It is a mistake to make 'invisible' synonymous with 'supernatural' because that contraction of meaning conceals from us the extent to which we, too, live in a world as invisible as Cotton Mather's – or Emily Dickinson's – and one which as much requires belief. Television does not give us human faces or human voices but only electronic simulations of them, selected and presented to us by interpreters. How shall we cross-check them? They make an invisible world.

[13]

Because beliefs are ways of separating out and patterning experience and thus making it available to us, they control us and, since to change beliefs is uncomfortable and even frightening, we willingly collaborate in processes which hold them in place and so protect us from the discrepancies and discontinuities which bring change. But we are not inert in this. It is not only true that history happens to us: we make it. The process is reciprocal.

If we turn from the historians' Salem to Emily Dickinson we can see in the following slight stanza the ways in which her interest in timelessness is intimately connected with, effectively, a withdrawal from participation and a submission to the control of circumstances.

> Witchcraft was hung, in History,
> But History and I
> Find all the Witchcraft that we need
> Around us, every Day – (# 1583)

When? Where? Out of what process, and with what consequences? Her mind does not work with such questions, so time is telescoped and made inaccessible to us as 'in History'. (There is no special significance in her capitals; generally she used them, as in German, for nouns.) It is possible to hang only witches, not witchcraft, so the first line is figurative and it is this figurativeness which facilitates one of the two slippages in the poem. When it first appears 'Witchcraft' means the malefic working of pins stuck into poppets, of ceremonies to deploy the powers of darkness to cause suffering or death; but 'Witchcraft' in the third line means the magic of the wonderful, the marvellous, the extraordinary, the benign. The poem turns on this pun. The other slippage is from 'History' meaning 'what is over and done with' to 'History' meaning 'the sum of all pasts, presents and futures'. The whole poem pivots on 'But': 'Witchcraft' is supposed to have survived the assault made on it in the past and 'History' to be truly shaped by what is innate in nature and not by something done long ago, once upon a time. We can have History without historical events. History does not change: around us, 'every Day', there is always 'Witchcraft'.

This stanza is one of those bright notes where she writes with the air of someone who has pulled out a plum, and in this it is not at all representative of her great poetry; but the position she takes in it is characteristic of her thought and indicates one of the reasons that some of her poems are difficult of approach. She wants to make human process (here, of hanging in the past but not hanging now) unimportant and a misperception. The witchcraft that is 'Around us, every Day' is so persistent and undefined that it would obviously be futile to try to do anything to it. It is beyond human power. Although its source is not located for us in the poem, plainly it is not witches. In the past there was (repellent) hanging, whereas there is now desirable magic. But the opposition in the poem is not really between now and then; it is between then and always. It is not that we now know better, having learned from experience. It is that the past provides clear evidence of the way that human history is superfluous and in contrast there is another sort of history which is real. The Olympian manner of 'History and I' marks not transcendental arrogance but her sense of the secondariness and the foreignness and the inertness of time when measured against the things which really matter.

What is this History which is untouched by history and which is the same every day?

Emily Dickinson spent her life seeking to live in its dimensions – though she used other names and frames for it than the one in the poem above ('history' is a rare word in her vocabulary). It is as though she came to a conviction about the way her life should be oriented and then began to explore the implications of that orientation. Her thought was not progressive. It was not nourished by and dependent on thoughts that she had had before. In this sense it stayed still to dilate the moment and the present book follows her in this by tracing her work not as a development but as an amplification. She had no project for her work. She did not carry through a purpose.

The effect of this has been to make her poems seem more than usually subject to the contingencies of circumstance – a chance meeting with a snake, or a hummingbird, a storm, some thoughts on a sunset. But when those poems are of great depth and turbulence and when, repeatedly, they revert to the same areas of disturbance, they encourage the view that there is an essential biographical pattern. Often commentators have felt that there is a story here if only they could find it, a novel of her life which would give them the generative springs.

Others have been less sanguine. She left behind nearly eighteen hundred lyrics – too many and too varied to be taken whole, and, though a tribute to the nomadic movement of her imagination, very uneven. Sometimes her poems are stringent, taut, fiercely alert; sometimes they are sentimental. Some show depths of insight and subtlety which set a reader's expectations high only for them to be betrayed by other work which, though it uses the same form and may set similar difficulties of approach, covers over the commonplace. Sometimes her tone is ironic, sometimes wistful; sometimes it is clamorous, sometimes plaintive, sometimes fulsome.

Faced with such multiplicity, R. P. Blackmur resorted to the desperate expedient of patronizing her thus:

> She was a private poet who wrote indefatigably as
> some women cook or knit. Her gift for words and the
> cultural predicament of her time drove her to poetry
> instead of antimacassars.[4]

This is to make her a poet of scraps, some of which are
accidentally brilliant; but Adrienne Rich is struggling
with the same essential difficulty when she says that
Emily Dickinson was many poets,[5] and so is David
Porter in his campaigning: 'We find, no matter with
what ingenuity we look, no solar system into whose
gravitational field all her experiences were attracted.'[6]
Given the challenge of her multiplicity, we can see why
Allen Tate's view[7] that she was caught up in Emerson's
war on Calvin has proved so durable. When we have an
individual poet whose own work seems to fragment, an
analogical claim is very persuasive. (R. P. Blackmur
scoffed at him: 'When he has got his image all made he
proceeds to sort out its component parts.')[8]

It is apparent that we have to cope with a number of
absences. Emily Dickinson is open to the making of
theses because she never prepared her poems for publication, and to this editorial absence must be added the
ambiguity and tentativeness of the dashes which she
generally used in preference to firmer, conventional
punctuation, and the lack of guidance which results
from her poems being untitled. Nor did she leave, in
either letter or essay, any extended prose discussion of
the way she thought about her art. We are denied even
secure texts or an unshakeable order of composition,
and the man who has done most to give them to us
observes of her poems: 'The dating of them is conjectural
and for the most part will always remain so.'[9]

The consequence is that inconvenient poems – there
may be a number, for one mood contradicts another –
may be neglected because any study of her work must
necessarily be so very selective. Yet a piece of little

[17]

merit on its own may receive much prominence because it illuminates some aspect of her thought, whereas a wonderful poem may be stubborn enough and opaque enough and so concentratedly itself as to make a reader doubt the illumination after all. We feel we need some secure centre which will enable us to determine what counts, and that seems to take us back to the story of her life.

I do not think that we should entirely relinquish this sense just because we cannot satisfy our curiosity. So figurative is Emily Dickinson's thought and so attracted by the riddle and the parable that it is difficult to believe that knowledge of, for example, the configurations of a frustrated love affair would not modify the contexts of some poems. So from her life-story we might receive significant help.

However, I think that underlying the biographical hope there has been a wish to provide what the verse does not provide and thus subtly to change its character by supplying its absences. We have little difficulty with time and place when she is writing about nature. The problems come with the space and span of poems which evoke states of feeling. We want to bring them under control by containing them under causes, yet I think that this shows an – understandable – reluctance to cross their imaginative threshold and occupy them on their own terms. It is as if we wanted to think of the poems themselves as acts of management and to derive some control-system from them.

We can see that our own acts of naming are acts of management which are achieved at the cost of severance. We refer, for example, to cedars, streams, birds' eggs and cloud formations as 'nature' and exclude from that word any possible reference to smoke-stacks. But why should we divide the world so as to form a grouping which will bring together worms and sunshine, or connect the rainbow and the scorpion? The word 'nature'

[18]

makes a choice for us. In doing this it both releases and inhibits by giving us the resources but also putting on us the limitations of certain inherited ways of dividing up our experience with words. If we see Emily Dickinson as a poet of revelations we can see that in some sense she must be a poet of those moments when the words run out. Her very practice is a contradiction: using words to evoke the wordless, using words made in history to point beyond history. If we see words as names and names as forms of control we can see that she is at a difficult intersection.

Those who see purposefulness as a masculine characteristic (who must labour to explain away purposeful women) and who see the absence of control over circumstances as essentially a feminine experience (seeming to deny that this could ever be a man's lot) would probably wish to make much at this juncture of Emily Dickinson's womanhood. Certainly questions of purposefulness and control underlie her work – and at a very deep level – but, at the moment, I do not see her as centrally representative of women: where she most demands she is unique: America's greatest nineteenth-century poet.

'I had no Monarch in my life, and cannot rule myself,' she maintained, 'and when I try to organise – my little Force explodes – and leaves me bare and charred –' (L 271). Do we not hope – however secretly – that poets will be prophets rather than note-makers, that they will have a sustaining vision? Yet here is Emily Dickinson declaring that she cannot meet that requirement, that the centre is absent. She has 'a Finless Mind' (L 319) and, as if to confirm the absent centre, 'My Business is Circumference.' (L 268)

It is as if she were prepared to register rather than shape. This seems to make her vulnerable to Blackmur's condescension – her poems merely the random products of diverse occasions – and it offers little guidance for a reader. If she could not find her own way through, how shall we? Her very standing and worth seem to be in question.

We must thread our way through paradoxes. The tone of some poems may be firm but the impression given by the whole work is that she is not confident. Edgy, nimble, restless, needing to keep her wits about her, she says many things and is not consistent, but this does not make her incoherent. What emerges is that she is a poet of passing away (death is one great form of this), of the elusive and the transient, and the fugitive, of what she called (# 812) 'a quality of loss'. Her great brilliance is with this and with the ominous, the vague, the threatening, the non-arrival, the not-quite-grasped, the not-quite-realized, the missing. At first sight she may not seem unusual in this, but most poets who consider these states do so in order to lament them. She, on the contrary, celebrates them, making a poetry of frissons and perturbations which others usually shrug off or seek to rationalize. So she will seem to stand things on their heads and say that, for example (# 745), 'Renunciation – is a piercing Virtue' or that loss is gain (# 968, # 1179).

Indeed, if we are not to recoil as from something wilful and unnatural, we need to look beneath the things she says for the insights on which they are grounded. ''Tis when / A Value struggle,' she wrote (# 806), that 'it exist –' and, obviously, this discourse of loss and gain is saturated with valuation which in turn involves questions of perspective. If we are to follow her logic we need to understand the heightened conscious-ness which – Emily Dickinson would maintain – goes with deprivation and the diminished consciousness which goes with repletion. 'The stimulus of Loss makes most Possession mean.' (L 364)

Why so? Well, she saw something enclosing and

insulating and contracting about possession, success, attainment, as if (# 1430) 'the Actual / Should disenthrall thy soul' whereas those defeated or denied were in her view expanded and opened out by their continuing aspiration, made more sensitive to the infinite and less locked in the circuit of their own circumscribed purposes. So:

> Satisfaction – is the Agent
> Of Satiety –
> Want – a quiet Commissary
> For Infinity.
>
> To possess, is past the instant
> We achieve the Joy –
> Immortality contented
> Were Anomaly. (# 1036)

Her work is not the product of an inability to live and relish but of intensity and ardour which she found significant in its very power and which she did not wish to see dissipated. For not being patient someone might find herself (# 534) 'waking in a Gnat's – embrace' when all the time there were 'Giants – further on –'. Desire, in all its varieties, meant something by itself, independent of its immediate objective, and loss or denial exposed this meaning. Hence she wrote, in a simple but carefully worded opposition which is a useful short-hand guide to her work (# 1349):

> I'd rather recollect a setting
> Than own a rising sun
>
> . . .
>
> Because in going is a Drama
> Staying cannot confer.

Once the implications of this are understood and her paradoxes steadily acquired like an idiom, then her work unfolds and we can see that the difficulty we have in managing the totality of it is intrinsic to a clash of

[21]

assumptions. It is as if we want it to be centripetal whereas it is centrifugal. At her best she enlarges our sense of being alive, but her position is a radical one because it involves undermining the very habit of sequence which is basic to many western thought processes: she challenges the idea of having objectives and seeking to reach them, of judging life by targets which are or are not attained. Such purposefulness, such targeting, makes someone vulnerable to circumstance, whereas her hope (in the event misplaced, in my view) is that someone who manages in different terms may be liberated:

> Superiority to Fate
> Is difficult to gain
> 'Tis not conferred of Any
> But possible to earn
>
> A pittance at a time
> Until to Her surprise
> The Soul with strict economy
> Subsist till Paradise. (# 1081)

By this austere discipline she makes herself the celebrant of sky-high aspiration, of unrealized potential in herself and in the world. She believes potential will always be bigger than its worldly accomplishment ('The Giant in the Human Heart was never met outside' (L 399)); but sometimes she is superbly happy and then she falters in this belief. At other times, possession, attainment, fulfilment, she mistrusts, like all the things she can get her hands on, because they seem illusory in face of the greater fulfilment of immortality and the intervening dispossession of death.

Is not this commendation of holding off special pleading? Is she not really making a virtue of a necessity? Moreover, is this not the supreme purposefulness, this postponement?

The answers lie not in the aphoristic commentaries which form much of her verse but in the quality of those other poems where something flits but is gone, or threatens but never actually shows its face, or promises, or glows but is missed. The answers are not in the neat and the clipped and the summed-up, but in the subtle, the delicate, the tenuous. I have already indicated that she is subject to history in that her attitude might change with circumstance. I try also to show that the contradiction in her poetry is that, though she maintained that 'True Poems flee' (# 1472), poems are a presence and a possession. To be so passive, so submissive to the great forces and fluctuations of life as she was, mistrusting what is known and consolidated and operating instead at the unstable periphery, is to live precariously. It is not surprising that she sometimes lapsed back into the security of the commonplace or the sentimental nor that her own varying assessment of where she stood should show her situation to be so volatile. She wanted to rid herself of time because she saw that as temporary and distorting (# 779):

> Rewarded Work —
>
> Has impetus of Gain —
> And impetus of Goal —
> There is no Diligence like that
> That knows not an Until —

The fact was that she put pencil to paper and entered history with her words.

We should respect this and not turn her into a static idea. I will give just two simple illustrations here. There is a daguerreotype likeness of the poet made when she was seventeen years old which can exercise a mischievous and potent effect on the mind of a reader (Emily for ever). Thus Archibald MacLeish has been

[23]

wittily chided for referring to her as 'this girl' when she died at the age of fifty-five.[10] Even more insidious is the tendency to become so mesmerized by the snapshot brevity of many of her pieces that we do not register alterations in her. The witchcraft poem I have quoted above has been attributed to 1883. It issues from a sense of herself in the world that would have been wholly impossible for her in some months of 1861 and 1862, yet the point of acknowledging this is not to offer to build up a chronology of development (supplying a sequence which her poems blur by fluctuation) but to resist the romantic attractions of a detached image.

The following is an example of what I mean:

> I must tell you about the *character* of Amherst. It is a lady whom the people call the *Myth*. She is a sister of Mr Dickinson, & seems to be the climax of all the family oddity. She has not been outside of her own house in fifteen years, except once to see a new church, when she crept out at night, & viewed it by moonlight. No one who calls upon her mother & sister ever see her, but she allows little children once in a great while, & one at a time, to come in, when she gives them cake or candy, or some nicety, for she is very fond of little ones. But more often she lets down the sweetmeat by a string, out of a window, to them. She dresses wholly in white, & her mind is said to be perfectly wonderful. She writes finely, but no one *ever* sees her. Her sister, who was at Mrs Dickinson's party, invited me to come & sing to her mother sometime . . . People tell me that the *myth* will hear every note – she will be near, but unseen . . . Isn't that like a book? So interesting.[11]

This description – fascinated, uncomprehending, of a stranger – comes from Mrs Mabel Loomis Todd who had then (1881) lived in Amherst a couple of months. (A year later she would fall in love with the poet's married brother, Austin; eight years after that she was to be largely responsible for editing the first selection of Emily Dickinson's poetry.) 'Like a book'? We can see why. The Emily Dickinson of this story plays the same part every day. She is not accessible to the listener in the to-and-fro of conversation, so she exists by reputation – that is, through intermediaries who are interpreters. She exists very much as the transcendent 'History' of her own poem exists, untouchably, and so becomes a projection of the imagination. The story of a genius secluded from the world (cruel world) is itself a romantic story and, unchecked, may feed the poems which are then conceded a marginal place in lives otherwise dedicated to more important things. Emily Dickinson probably encouraged such myths as her way of managing her life. The most difficult element to accept and to understand in one so reflective is the element of the performer.

She was born on 10 December 1830, in Amherst, Massachusetts, then a town of 2631, and she died there on 15 May 1886, by which time it had grown by about 1500. Her grandfather, Samuel Fowler Dickinson, a lawyer, was largely responsible for the founding of Amherst College as a bulwark of religious orthodoxy against the liberalizing tendencies of Harvard, and her father, Edward, and her older brother, Austin, also lawyers, became in turn its treasurer.

Emily Dickinson's first home was in half of an impos-ing dwelling called the Homestead, reportedly the town's first brick house, which her father shared initi-ally with her grandfather who had built it. In 1840 the family moved to a house in North Pleasant Street which was close to the town's West Cemetery, but in 1855 they moved back to the Homestead, this time occupying the whole house. She never moved again. Across Main Street was the Dickinson Meadow where she might have found 'a Boggy Acre' to see 'A narrow

Fellow in the Grass' or the frog whose public croaking she mocked in # 288 – the point is not to find real locations to substitute for the transformations of the imagination but to suggest the potential range of experience within the immediate area. The train of her 'I like to see it lap the Miles' (# 585) could have been conceived on one which ran on rails only a few hundred yards from her house.

She boasted – the right word, I think – that she had never seen the sea (# 1052, L 1004), but she spent two periods of some months away from home in seaboard Boston in 1864 and 1865 receiving medical treatment. Her hesitation about accepting an invitation there in 1866 ('I had promised to visit my Physician for a few days in May, but Father objects because he is in the habit of me' L 316) became the famous, resounding: 'I do not cross my Father's ground to any House or town' (L 330), of 1869. Previous crossing of her father's ground had taken her in 1855 to Washington and to Philadelphia, and, from September 1847 to August 1848, to Mount Holyoke Female Seminary in South Hadley, but she preferred home – with increasing warmth – and in 1863 she was being teased about this by a family friend who wrote to her brother:

> . . . & to the Queen Recluse my especial sympathy – that she has 'overcome the world' – Is it really true that they ring 'Old Hundred' & 'Aleluia' perpetually, in heaven – ask her; and are dandelions, asphodels, & Maiden's *vows*? the standard flowers of the ethereal?[12]

To be prepared to be so robustly jocular with her about something so sensitive when her letters to him show great trust suggests that he knew something about her which we do not.

What we have, instead, in the awed emphasis of anecdote, is the story of a woman who, increasingly until it became an invariable habit, wore white; who sometimes refused to see visitors, sending them instead of her company a glass of wine or some flowers and perhaps an accompanying poem; and who seems to have become less and less disposed to go into public places, shy – or reluctant – of encountering neighbours or strangers who did not belong to her close-knit circle of family and friends – a refusal of the casual which included the quirky habit of getting other people to address most of the envelopes for the many letters that she sent. Sometimes when visitors were received she spoke to them through a half-opened door and not directly face to face. When Mrs Todd, who described 'the Myth', did sing at the Homestead she was heard from a room above. Stories of oddity attract with magnetic power other corroborative stories of oddity but without giving insight into whether she was very timid or mark-edly aloof, or both. How *many* people received the genteel brush-off of wine or flowers on a silver tray? How *many* people were spoken to with the door ajar, as if at a Roman Catholic confessional? We can form only the crudest idea of the pattern of her daily life, of what was typical in it and what exceptional.

Certainly, she seems to have taken further than most the wish not to be disturbed that probably we all have from time to time, but I am not persuaded that this was chiefly for the sake of her poetry (the reason often offered). She wrote less though she became more and more retiring. Rather, I think, her privacy was a means of carefully controlling the relationships she had with other people, as if each encounter were so full and stimulating an occasion – if it were not the other sort, a tiresome and useless distraction – that she needed to check it.

Her own behaviour is in conspicuous contrast to that of her father. Could there have been a more public man? His political career took him, in 1838 and again in 1873, as an elected representative, to the General Court of Massachusetts; to the State Senate in 1842 and 1843; and, in 1852 as delegate, to the National Whig convention; and culminated in that year in his election as Representative to the United States Congress. He was Amherst's most prominent citizen, active in bringing in the new (1853) Amherst–Belchertown Railroad, active in introducing the telegraph, a life director of the Home Mission Society and trustee of the Northampton hospital. Town father, pillar of the church, LLD of Amherst College, 'There was hardly a civic project in Amherst, from the founding of the Massachusetts Agricultural College to the establishment of the local water works, in which Edward Dickinson was not a central figure.'[13] It was he who took charge of fighting a bad fire in the town in July 1851 and he who showed proprietorial confidence in his social position by using the church bell not to alert people to another one but to summon the town to see a spectacular display of northern lights.

So sharp is the contrast between father and daughter that we can see that he made a sort of proxy world of public affairs available for her scrutiny. Moreover, the idea of her being cut off from the world is difficult to reconcile with the list of approximately a hundred people who had letters from her during her life – the more so when we notice that two of the closest of those correspondents were Dr J. G. Holland, editor of *Scribner's Monthly,* and – closer still – Samuel Bowles, editor of the *Springfield Daily Republican.* She read the newspapers. She knew what was going on.

However, if talking about things in letters and writing about things in poetry be taken as the decisive guides, it is evident that what mattered most to her was either vaster or else more intimate. Outside her family there were a number of men in her life, some known, some known of, some conjectured. At least

twice she was deeply in love. On the second occasion
the man was a family friend of long-standing, the – to
many others – forbidding Massachusetts Supreme
Court Judge, Otis Lord. This was late in her life and
later in his, after he had been widowed. On what may
have been the first occasion of love (rumour talks of
other possibilities), the major one for her poetry, we do
not know who she fell in love with or what his response
was, but he seems to have been married. Her feelings
were in crisis in the winter of 1861 through to 1862 and
it is traditional to associate this with the announced
May departure of the Reverend Charles Wadsworth of
Philadelphia (whom she had heard preach and who
visited her) for the church of Calvary, San Francisco
(to which some have seen an allusion in the 'Calvary'
of her poetry), though Sam Bowles' departure for Europe
in April 1862 (he returned in November) nearly co-
incides with this. (His were the teasing remarks I
quoted earlier.) Whatever may have been the explanation for it, we are left with the sense of a survived trial
of some length and of very great depth. On the written
evidence it was the crisis of her life and poems of great
quality poured from her in astonishing energy of
creativity.

During it she wrote to a complete stranger, a former
Unitarian minister turned literary man, Thomas
Wentworth Higginson, ostensibly for advice about her
work. Can poetry and life be kept separate? Twice
subsequently she told him that he saved her life that
year (L 330 & 621) and, however hyperbolic, this is not
the language of someone grateful for instruction in
metrics. If we may believe that she had some desperate
need, there is no clear guide as to whether that need
was bound up with her poetry or whether poetry was
the relatively impersonal medium which she could use
as cover to satisfy it – or even that she knew what that

need was. Her brother Austin said that she definitely posed in her letters to Higginson[14] and it is interesting to have this confirmation of what is evident when they are compared with the more open and fluent ones which went, for example, to her cousins, Frances and Louise Norcross. Her posing extended as far as presenting herself as a mere beginner when she had by this time written not the two or three poems of her admission but some three hundred, and insinuating a picture of herself isolated in her family and needing sympathy when there was no place which she preferred to home and, when the test came, she would not meet Higginson anywhere else. What her requirements of him were it is difficult to know since it is hard to believe that he made any difference to her poetry. In letters to him she generally signed herself 'Your scholar' or, occasionally, 'Dickinson' and at times she referred to him as 'Master'. There is an additional interest in this role-playing because of the so-called 'Master' letters (L 187, 233, 248 – the last two of these tortured) which she drafted to an anonymous correspondent whom she evidently loved before she knew Higginson.

Before he had met her (1869, L 330a) Higginson felt that he could not reach her because she enshrouded herself in a 'fiery mist'. He has been mocked for asking for a photograph of a woman whom, it is suggested, he should have realized he knew well from her correspondence; but if we read the correspondence we can see why he asked for the likeness: 'I had no portrait, now, but am small, like the Wren, and my Hair is bold, like the Chestnut Bur – and my eyes, like the Sherry in the Glass, that the Guest leaves –' (L 268). Delightful this may be – it is meant to be – but it does not allow the man to make up his own mind. Emily Dickinson was intent on being elusive, and to seize with eagerness – or relief – on her disclaimer: 'When I state myself, as the

Representative of the Verse – it does not mean – me – but a supposed person' (L 268) is to disregard her feigning.

Higginson kept up a correspondence with her that lasted till her death and when in 1870 and 1873 he went to see her in Amherst *he* had no difficulty in being received. After her death he collaborated with Mrs Todd in editing the first selection of her poems. During her life, only weeks after her first writing, he was away fighting in the Civil War as colonel of the First Carolina Volunteers. His struggle against slavery involved him in membership of the Secret Six who planned with John Brown the Harper's Ferry Raid of 16 October 1859, and he was vigorous in other liberal causes. Mocking his inadequacies as a reader of poetry and literary mentor has been a frequent pleasure amongst the poet's biographers, though suggestions for an alternative adequate to her distinctiveness have been less forthcoming, as have speculations about what would have happened if *he* had gone to *her* for help instead. Plainly, he also was a public man.

Few details need be added to suggest the orbit of Emily Dickinson's domestic life. She was much occupied by home. This was expanded by friendship – for a time passionate, at others strained – with Susan Huntington Gilbert ('Sue') who excited her greatly and to whose sharp mind and forceful personality she was always sensitive. Sue married Emily Dickinson's brother Austin in July 1856 and they moved into the Evergreens, the house next door to the Homestead. The stream of visitors drawn to the Homestead by Edward Dickinson's prominent position tended to flow now towards the Evergreens as the town's centre of society, but Austin's marriage was not happy. He remained close to his sister and also to Lavinia ('Vinnie'), Emily Dickinson's younger sister who became fiercely antagonistic to Sue. 'What makes a few of us so different from others?' Emily once asked Austin (L 118), and she asked it approvingly, marvelling elsewhere: 'How extraordinary that Life's large Population contain so few of power to us.' (L 275)

Edward Dickinson died in 1874, being survived by his wife who within a year began to need much nursing, the main requirement of the two sisters' lives until her death in 1882. After Emily's own death in 1886 Vinnie destroyed letters as bidden but she had no direction as to what to do with the many hundreds of poems she discovered in a locked box, a majority of them loosely tied into packets of four to six sheets of folded paper. Sue had received 276 poems, Higginson 102, Sam Bowles and his wife 37, Dr Holland and his wife 35, and others were spread amongst other correspondents. Seven poems of the now recovered total found a way into print in Emily Dickinson's lifetime – all anonymously – and of that total only 24 were titled by the poet, usually in an accompanying note. Publication of her work began in 1890, but it was not until 1955 that an authoritative edition appeared. The poet had left it to chance – or History.

In approaching her work we face, then, the contradiction that few have been less interested in temporal circumstances than she and that, at her finest, she prized those nameless moments when she seemed, with awe, to be at the edge of the eternal, yet we know about them only because she entered history, used the communal language, and was not simply a receptor but one who took initiatives as a creator. The kind of retreat we have from agency in the passive 'was hanged' of her witchcraft stanza sometimes carries through to the extent of her using uninflected verbs as if she could make an art of the infinitive. 'Be seen', 'arise', 'remit' are examples (from 'Further in Summer than the Birds'). In context are they past, present, or future? Are they first, second, or third person? They seem to wish to escape from time. Yet she could not. We have her work because of a series of interventions in history of which hers was the first and to which, in selecting and appraising as readers, we add another.

# II

# Theatre of the World

'We are here, Your Honor, precisely to discover what no one has ever seen.'

Arthur Miller, *The Crucible,* Act 3

When Emily Dickinson was buried she was in a white coffin carried on a special bier by six of the men who worked in her father's grounds. It is worth recalling this, because though she cooked and worked in the garden, the essential formality of the relationship she had with the outside world could be preserved only because there were always people such as Maggie Maher to answer the door if Vinnie did not, and others who would take letters to the post. The elegant austerity of her life was not a solitary but a collaborative effort.

Cultural traditions, too, are an expression of the shared. She was at the disturbed confluence of two very powerful ones: of that New England Puritanism that had once hanged witches, which was waning, and of that New England Romanticism which, in the person of Ralph Waldo Emerson, once came to stay next door at the Evergreens. 'Her peculiar burden,' writes Albert Gelpi, 'was to be a Romantic poet with a Calvinist's sense of things; to know transitory ecstasy in a world tragically fallen and doomed.'[1] In the slight poem (# 285) where she accepts, in a famous phrase, that she sees 'New Englandly' she

[34]

means simply that she is accustomed to robins, buttercups, autumn nuts and snow rather than cuckoos and daisies; but she might have referred to the fact that it was the hymnbooks of Isaac Watts which gave her the models for her verse forms or that the descendants of Calvin had set a frame for her thought. She might write of the rest of her family: 'They will all go but me, to the usual meeting-house, to hear the usual sermon; the inclemency of the storm so kindly detaining me . . .' (L 77) but the legacy of such sermons was with her for life.

It originated with John Calvin in sixteenth-century Geneva, found some temporary welcome in England and a firmer one in Scotland, but eventually had to be exported to America where, under the secular pressure of nationhood, it became, reluctantly, less fierce.

Words such as 'intolerant' need some scrutiny (is it a bad thing to be intolerant of Nazism?), but, notwithstanding its many very different English variants,[2] it was intolerant. Two Americans observe:

> The Puritans were assured that they alone knew the exact truth, as it was contained in the written word of God, and they were fighting to enthrone it in England and to extirpate utterly and mercilessly all other pretended versions of Christianity. When they could not succeed at home, they came to America, where they could establish a society in which the one and only truth should reign forever. There is nothing so idle as to praise the Puritans for being in any sense conscious or deliberate pioneers of religious liberty.[3]

It was intolerant, perhaps, because separation was one of its essential principles. It conceived of mankind as divided into the chosen, 'the Elect', whom God had selected for redemption and who were the company of

[35]

the Saints, and the Damned. Calvin had taught that neither group controlled its destiny. The Elect were powerless to earn salvation by doing good works, they were dependent entirely on God's gift of grace; and the Damned could do nothing to recover themselves. Must not those who opposed or sought to modify the faith be amongst the Damned?

Such a static system might seem to be entirely without moral imperatives. Why should someone live a good life if his reward were to be damnation? Why need a Saint behave morally if his salvation were guaranteed? A teaching which left life so totally in the hands of God might seem to take away all initiative for action and be simply descriptive. In fact, Puritanism released the energy of uncertainty. If the basic division left people with nothing more attractive than a gambler's chance with no dice to throw, their very ignorance of their destiny was a powerful incentive to behave as if they were saved. Sobriety and rectitude in public, scrupulous examination of conscience in private were the indispensable requirements of a life that was preparing itself for the appalling rigour of Judgement. Of course, people would wish to repudiate sin – their own and others'. Of course they would wish to repudiate the Damned – in order to strengthen their sense of being amongst the Elect. God judged and punished. Believers did likewise.

We can see that what made uncertainty possible and thus what made Puritanism into a dynamic system was a double scale of time and a dual sense of place – both of which show powerfully in Emily Dickinson's poetry.

Human beings live with time-bound minds. They are told to believe that in the past Adam sinned and was expelled from Eden and that, in consequence, they are born in a fallen state. The state of nature is a state of

[36]

original sin. The past is thus firm and known and true universally: we all begin on the outside, out of Eden. The future, however, is personal, for we face the separation called Judgement where some go one way and some another. If the possibility of Damnation makes that prospect appalling, the possibility of Bliss makes it deeply attractive: in the future we might recover the Garden, or we might be shut out of it for ever. However, no matter what the proportions of fear and hope which this situation encourages in the believer, it is clear that it is in the future that the deepest reality lies. There we shall know the truth about ourselves which is concealed on earth. There we shall come to rest, for there humanity's time and God's timelessness intersect; and we can surely see the earth as only a place of transit. The future is our target. The future is the reference point and mark we steer by now. It is the future that ultimately makes meaning since it is the realest real we shall ever know. Emily Dickinson kept this as a major emphasis and orientation. It helps explain her relative lack of interest in the past and a certain restlessness about the status of the present.

It follows from this obsessive interest in future destiny that the present is subordinate and may even be felt to be an irritating distraction. The present is something to be used – as a means to an end. It is not something to be relished. It may set up false perspectives, it may generate false values. We should not be in love with this world, we should try to get through it as quickly as possible. 'Men huddle up their lives here,' wrote a visitor to Boston from England in 1686, 'as a thing of no use, and wear it out like an old suit, the faster the better.'[4] Puritanism does not live in the present. Puritanism is constantly moving. This, too, is marked in Emily Dickinson's thought.

But this is to think on a human and temporal scale.

For God, time does not exist. Human beings with their time-bound minds could surely not conceive of such a world except in negatives – a world without sequence, a world without cause and effect, with no past and no future. So we fumble in the attempt and produce a sort of compression of time into an instant. 'Forever – is composed of Nows –' Emily Dickinson wrote (# 624). In that instant Now of human approximation are to be found all pasts and all futures, all knowledge – all destinies therefore. God, unlike humanity, knows where we will finish up before we start off since in his sight human beings simply are and time (as in Emily Dickinson's poetry) is another name for restricted knowledge. This is why humanity is said to be predestined.

The struggle is thus to leave behind the temporal perspective of fallen earth and to move towards the perspective of the eternal. It is a struggle which involves a dual sense of place.

The real world is a heavenly-diabolic one, of naked contest between a victorious God and a scheming but defeated Satan – a world (to use temporal thought) where the outcome of that struggle has been revealed. However, we live in this one, this place of transit which, though it appears substantial, is actually deceptive; and in this one the outcome of the struggle is unknown to us. It is in this sense that I think we can see life as a performance and the world as a theatre in which we play out our divinely assigned parts but without knowing what the script holds for each person. Moreover, since the real world is elsewhere and this is a world of illusions, we all in some way wear the masks of temporal life. It seems inconceivable that good should feign being evil, but in this theatre of Satan's scheming we must expect evil to feign being good. We must be wary, suspect deception (harmless old women may be

Satan's agents), try to get through to the real. This is the double-natured world of Puritanism – and of Hawthorne's novels and stories – of public front and secret truth. It is a world of signs and pointers, a world that needs to be read – the world of Herman Melville.

Disaffected, Emily Dickinson came to abandon any external connection with the meeting house, but a letter of 1854 when she was twenty-three records the impact it had made:

> The minister to-day, not our own minister, preached about death and judgement, and what would become of those, meaning Austin and me, who behaved improperly – and somehow the sermon scared me, and father and Vinnie looked very solemn as if the whole was true, and I would not for worlds have them know that it troubled me, but I longed to come to you, and tell you all about it, and learn how to be better. He preached such an awful sermon though, that I didn't much think I should ever see you again until the Judgement Day, and then you would not speak to me, according to his story. The subject of perdition seemed to please him, somehow. (L 175)

For her the sermon evidently worked on two levels. We can see it gripping her imagination at the same time that she doubts its authenticity – 'his story', she writes, and she observes the incongruity of its seeming to please him.

The apparent impossibility which shows there of connecting the apocalyptic prospect of Judgement with anything familiar shows, too, in a letter to Sue earlier that year. She rushes for home, and: 'How I did wish for you – how, for my own dear Vinnie – how for Goliah [sic], or Samson – to pull the whole church down, requesting Mr Dwight to step into Miss Kingsbury's, until the dust was past!' (L 154) How could she live simultaneously in the worlds of Goliath and Mr Dwight?

[39]

In 1846 she had hoped that 'my heart will willingly yield itself to Christ, and that my sins will be all blotted out of the book of remembrance.' How sad it would be 'for one of our number to go to the dark realms of wo, where is the never dying worm and the fire which no water can quench, and how happy if we may be one unbroken company in heaven.' (L 10) The fifteen-year-old had had the same difficulty in trying to reconcile the fiery world of words which worked on her imagination with her happy and familiar experiences. She never did reconcile them. However she might characterize them – as 'mind' or 'belief' or 'ideal' or 'words' opposed to 'experience' or 'life' or 'earth' – and however she might deny or denigrate one of them, she was gripped by both. She lived in a familiar world that was vulnerable to incursions of the strange and she was awed and thrilled by the contradiction of the meeting. As religious revivals swept Amherst and, at Mount Holyoke, as she was asked to place herself either amongst those who 'had hope' or those who were 'without hope' one unintended effect of the preaching which she heard would be to distance the future in its scale and importance and drama from the humdrum mundane.

In one poem I think we have a piece recording the moment of impact. I read this as her response to a sermon:

> He fumbles at your Soul
> As Players at the Keys
> Before they drop full Music on –
> He stuns you by degrees –
> Prepares your brittle Nature
> For the Ethereal Blow
> By fainter Hammers – further heard –
> Then nearer – Then so slow
> Your Breath has time to straighten –
> Your Brain – to bubble Cool –
> Deals – One – imperial – Thunderbolt –

That scalps your naked Soul –
When Winds take Forests in their Paws –
The Universe – is still –

She is excited here by demonstrated power. Fully aware
of the way she is being manipulated – first the fumbling
preliminaries, then the full effort; first the preparation, little by little, then closer; then, reassuringly,
slower; then the thunderbolt – she enjoys the drama.
The whole poem is expectant, thrilling to the performance of its own arousal, yet passive. It is unstrug-
gling as, in the contradiction of the last lines, a whole
bystanding universe goes still in awe.

It is as though Emily Dickinson had found in the
awesome forces of nature an indication of the scale and
power she associated with the thrilling dramas of the
pulpit. We find the same passivity in the face of those
forces in a quite different poem, but the terms of
parables are simplifying terms. This is no poetry of
social nuance.

A Solemn thing within the Soul
To feel itself get ripe –
And golden hang – while farther up –
The Maker's Ladders stop –
And in the Orchard far below –
You hear a Being – drop –

A Wonderful – to feel the Sun
Still toiling at the Cheek
You thought was finished –
Cool of eye, and critical of Work –
He shifts the stem – a little –
To give your Core – a look –

But solemnest – to know
Your chance in Harvest moves
A little nearer – Every Sun
The Single – to some lives.

[41]

To be thunderstruck, to be harvested, is to be done to in both cases. The attraction of the poem is in the boldness which risks comparing the ripening of fruit in an orchard with the approach of death and possible immortal life and the delicacy which sustains both the image and the reality as occurring under the same universal 'Sun'. (She also risks omitting repetition of 'thing within the Soul' after 'Wonderful' and compressing the idea that for some *this* day's sun is their last into the one word 'single'.) But what does the ripening mean outside the terms of the parable? If we do not ask, it is because we are obedient to the sensuous pleasures of sunbathing and because there is enjoyment, too, in having responsibility for the whole affair taken by somebody else. It might be very agreeable to live in a figure of speech; and this, after all, was what the word preached in sermons had offered her. As she wrote of her Bible-reading, 'I wished that that wonderful world had commenced, which makes such promises.' (L 185)

However often she might feel intimidated by that wonderful world, it is striking that she quickly abandoned some of the Calvinist options for characterizing it. For all that she says, tremblingly, in some early letters (including those quoted above), there are two major omissions from her poetry. The first is sin and the second is Satan. In one poem she does talk about herself as 'spotted' (# 964) but this is only to have it brushed aside in a not very profound piece of play-acting and in one of the three instances where she uses 'sin' it is to scoff at it as 'a distinguished Precipice / Others must resist' (# 1545). (The other two, in # 801 and # 1460, are negligible.) In general, hers is not poetry of a moral dimension. She is not troubled by guilt.

In similar vein, she describes a light-hearted life, disregarding its burden of original sin and frittered away in *not* redeeming the time:

> She died at play,
> Gambolled away
> Her lease of spotted hours,
> Then sank as gaily as a Turk
> Upon a Couch of flowers.

Surely some divine calamity must follow? Surely some fearsome retribution? Hardly.

> Her ghost strolled softly o'er the hill
> Yesterday, and Today,
> Her vestments as the silver fleece –
> Her countenance as spray. (# 75)

The poem is thus taking an amused pleasure in the absence of such old bogies, but we will not make much of it unless we know that they once existed.

Satan? The Devil? He is seen as a bit of type-casting, a military man, 'the Brigadier' (# 1545) and he is worth one other joke. It is a pity he cannot change, 'Because he has ability' and would make a very good friend (# 1479). The trouble is that he is so utterly disloyal. She says, in a piece of wit recalling implicitly that he was once God's angel, if only he would give up disloyalty he would be 'thoroughly divine'.

However, the assurance that produces these *jeux d'esprit* does not come from a contemptuous post-religious mind. On the contrary, Puritanism has been taken very seriously, but now the balance has shifted away from condemnation and in favour of innocence. The moment of clarity when the real (heavenly) world of Noon exposes this world is likened in an early poem to a clearing of the air beneath a high vantage point:

> When we stand on the tops of Things –
> And like the Trees, look down –
> The smoke all cleared away from it –
> And Mirrors on the scene –

[43]

Just laying light – no soul will wink
Except it have the flaw –
The Sound ones, like the Hills – shall stand –
No Lightning, scares away –

The Perfect, nowhere be afraid –
They bear their dauntless Heads,
Where others, dare not go at Noon,
Protected by their deeds –

The Stars dare shine occasionally
Upon a spotted World –
And Suns, go surer, for their Proof,
As if an Axle, held – (# 242)

The basic distinction in the poem is between obscurity
and brilliantly clarifying light. When the smoke moves
away nothing stops the (heavenly) sun shining into the
earth's mirroring pools of water, testing observers. It is
a Judgement. Those with flawed souls are dazzled
('wink') but 'the Sound', 'The Perfect' are (twice) not
frightened but 'stand' whereas others who are shielded
only by their good 'deeds' will not risk the light. This
imperfect world, for all its obscurity, is 'occasionally'
feebly illuminated. However weak such 'stars', this is a
presence of light, a witness to the greater fact of the
sun ('Suns' because each day has one) in whose arrival
we can feel greater confidence because some light has
been maintained (the 'Proof' of the last stanza). The
poem is thoroughly Puritan in its division of people on
other than earned merit and in its expectation of light
which is only hinted at now. Yet it does not issue in
ideas of duty and guilt but in security. The interest is
not in sin or morality or even obedience but in surety,
'As if an Axle, held –', and that is made to depend on
circumstances grounded in laws rather than in the
capricious authority of a personal God. This preoccu-

pation with security is recurrent in her poetry, though
she is ambivalent about it.

For the orthodox Puritan it was heresy to maintain
that men and women could merit heaven by their good
works ('Protected by their deeds'). The initiative had to
stay with God and the gift of his grace. However,
Increase Mather had found that they might *prepare* for
salvation (just as his son, Cotton, found a device to end
the Salem witch trials): he advised that 'they should do
such things as have a tendency to cause them to Believe'.[5] Perry Miller describes the process:

> A teleological universe, wherein men were expected to
> labor for the glory of God, wherein they were to seek
> not their own ends but solely those appointed by Him,
> was imperceptibly made over into a universe in which
> men could trust themselves even to the extent of
> commencing their own conversions, for the sake of
> their own well-being, and God could be expected to
> reward them with eternal life. Even while professing
> the most abject fealty to the Puritan Jehovah, the
> Puritan divines in effect dethroned Him. The fate of
> New England, in the original philosophy, depended
> upon God's providence; the federal theology circum-
> scribed providence by tying it to the behaviour of the
> saints; then, with the extension of the field of be-
> haviour through the elaboration of the work of prepar-
> ation, the destiny of New England was taken out of the
> hands of God and put squarely into the keeping of the
> citizens.[6]

Emily Dickinson's life repeats in miniature this process of enfranchisement and her poetry may be seen as
a record of the work of preparation; but, of course, it
ran outside orthodox channels. The sense that the
world is an obscure place full of secrets where reality is
hidden and daily life is a riddle vies with another that
the Elect must be Redeemed in some sense already,

must have a hold on heaven now. Life is over-full with potential that may not be realized but which nonetheless is real. We can reread Calvinism as a myth about states of awareness which repeats but reverses the myth of the Fall. Adam, innocent and unaware, ate the apple and knew. Fallen man, ignorant and blundering in a dark world, will at a future moment see. Heaven will be a revelation.

Must he wait?

There is a Quaker answer to that question, and for insisting on inner illumination, four of those who gave it and refused exile for giving it were hanged on Boston Common. Once shed the restraints of doctrine and there is no knowing where the spirit may guide. So far does Emily Dickinson go down the road of independence that not only do the manoeuvres and stratagems of religious orthodoxy – cliché-ridden, intimidatory preaching; dogmatic theology; biblical fundamentalism – receive a very caustic reception from her but, except for a period in the 1860s, God seems to have gone to the peripheries of her heaven. Personal adoration of him is not something to be associated with her. He does not feel very close. He was for her at times a licensing authority, at times a feature of landscape or an impressive name. Characteristic is her phrase (# 1090) 'And God, for a Frontier', a usage which contrasts markedly with, for example, George Herbert's in 'The Agonie':

> Love is that liquor sweet and most divine,
> Which my God feels as bloude; but I, as wine.

Emily Dickinson may have been a supplicant in one or two poems but we are not given the sense of an interest in God's feelings or made to believe in her experience of a relationship – the experience signified by Herbert's simple 'my'.

There are certainly some poems which support

William Sherwood's persuasively argued view that in 1862 she went through a religious conversion, but we have to say that either it was temporary or else it had such unorthodox implications that it is not worth calling it that. Repeatedly she writes as if the ideas of Calvinism were ones available to her rather than ones she actually inhabited, as if they were true but she did not belong to them. We see this in a poem on the Resurrection. She is trying to absorb the idea and to make it significant for herself. She reasons. She deduces. If cause, then surely effect. There is a gigantic marshalling of all the dead for Judgement. Dust lives, atoms are given faces again (some years later she would wonder about that):

> No Crowd that has occurred
> Exhibit – I suppose
> That General Attendance
> That Resurrection – does –
>
> Circumference be full –
> The long restricted Grave
> Assert her Vital Privilege –
> The Dust – connect – and live –
>
> On Atoms – features place –
> All Multitudes that were
> Efface in the Comparison –
> As Suns – dissolve a star –
>
> Solemnity – prevail –
> Its Individual Doom
> Possess each separate Consciousness –
> August – Absorbed – Numb –
>
> What Duplicate – exist –
> What Parallel can be –
> Of the Significance of This –
> To Universe – and Me? (# 515)

It is an awesome subject, and it ought to be central to the Calvinist imagination. If crowds are impressive in their numbers, none will ever impress more than this one. Could there be anything on a grander scale, or of more crucial moment? But there lies the problem: the scale and the crux have only a fortuitous connection. The last line shows clearly what the penultimate stanza also reveals: the poem does not have an agreed centre. The flicker of wit that crosses the poem's third line (being compulsory, 'General Attendance' *would* be high) and the tendency to identify this crowd with the dead rather than with the living, too, keep it at an observer's distance. In the subtly false comparison of Suns against a star 'Multitudes that were' are contrasted with this multitude; but this multitude is not separate from and in competition with those: it incorporates them. By its very nature we are all in it. It is *us*. Yet Emily Dickinson is evidently thinking of it as *them* for it has a collective significance to the others, the 'Universe', and a private significance to 'Me'. Her 'Universe and Me' mistake resembles her 'History – and I' mistake and is similar to the blunder 'Britain and Europe' or 'The United States and California'. It betrays a distinction of interests when the explicit claim is for unity. What has possessed her imagination is the public momentousness of unparalleled scale which gives unity to the crowd, but its analysed 'Significance' is 'Individual' and 'separate' and consists in division. Why it is universally significant (beyond the fact that it affects everyone) she does not say. Someone for whom the Resurrection was self-evidently of unparalleled importance would either not have declared it or else would have explored that importance. The poem is recessional.

It deals, that is, with a location of Calvinism, but without its plan. It presents a moment, but without action. It has no outcome. It is a situation immobilized in any case but aided in its stasis by (once again) uninflected verbs.

We can see that this is imagining which comes from a mind not previously inspected for doctrinal orthodoxy and church approval. It serves itself (and incidentally makes a reader realize how coercive and purposeful ideas of the afterlife usually are). At the same time the very firmness of such orthodox patterns can itself be reassuring.

In another treatment of the Judgement theme we begin comfortably settled in something like a cliché of Sunday School art or Victorian religious illustration:

> Departed – to the Judgement –
> A Mighty Afternoon –
> Great Clouds – like Ushers – leaning –
> Creation – looking on –

The show is about to begin? This is the way a certain sort of sepia-illustrated religious tradition might expect the event to take place, with external attributions of awe from the appropriate cloudscape in a spectacle remote from the deepest concerns of our inner lives. The scene arouses some curiosity since there is as yet no one to be judged and no judge but merely the suggestion of the formal ritual of a court trial. That is the way it proceeds, with just enough to indicate the arcane process of something legal being transacted, of terms being met and documents being amended: 'The Flesh – Surrendered – Cancelled –'. But then the scene is grammatically disrupted: 'The Bodiless – begun – / Two Worlds – like Audiences – disperse – / And leave the Soul – alone –' (# 524). A bodiless what? But *what* is exactly the question the situation engenders – life? death? The nature of the existence of the soul departed

[49]

is now out of reach of vocabulary, out of reach, too, of the assuring comfort of forensic ritual. We are left uncertain about whether we have had the judgement or whether the judgement is now about to begin, but the isolation is disconcerting indeed when the imagined drama of religious tradition simply dissolves as if it were quite inadequate to represent the real truth.

Others amongst her poems also unnerve by removing assuring circumstance. In the poem 'I died for Beauty', death for beauty is not the poem's core.

> I died for Beauty – but was scarce
> Adjusted in the Tomb
> When One who died for Truth, was lain
> In an adjoining Room –
>
> He questioned softly 'Why I failed'?
> 'For Beauty', I replied –
> 'And I – for Truth – Themself are One –
> We Brethren, are', He said –
>
> And so, as Kinsmen, met at Night –
> We talked between the Rooms –
> Until the Moss had reached our lips –
> And covered up – our names –

It pauses on a dash, ready, we might suppose, to go in a Keatsian direction, when it is disrupted by a veering 'but' which makes us reflect on how perfunctory death for beauty was, how difficult, in the abstract, to relate to. 'Death for truth' is no better, but death for beauty and death for truth get into conversation with some speed, if a little initial uncertainty in case the opening enquiry be an indiscreet one. The deceased comparing case histories, perhaps we shall have something like the growlers of Thomas Hardy's 'Channel Firing' discussing the state of the world? Or perhaps death-for-beauty and death-for-truth are tokens still to be spent by the poet? Neither is the case. There is another displacement of the poem's centre. The overwhelming moss denies the importance of the conversation about the kinship of truth and beauty without claiming the place for itself. It is not the substance of the poem which carries its charge but its change in modes. It begins in a highly symbolic Gothic fantasy which is then intersected by the naturalism of weathering tombstones. We might have expected a discourse, we have witnessed instead a very familiar but inexplicable act of encroachment. The world has changed behind the words. How, after all, could 'adjustment' be expected in a tomb? The range of meaning was wrong. Not adjustment, but – we do not know what. Death is not the kind of experience to allow us to know.

'Because I could not stop for Death' works through another set of lethal pleasantries.

> Because I could not stop for Death –
> He kindly stopped for me –
> The Carriage held but just Ourselves –
> And Immortality.
>
> We slowly drove – He knew no haste
> And I had put away
> My labor and my leisure too,
> For His Civility –
>
> We passed the School, where Children strove
> At Recess – in the Ring –
> We passed the Fields of Gazing Grain –
> We passed the Setting Sun –
>
> Or rather – He passed Us –
> The Dews drew quivering and chill –
> For only Gossamer, my Gown –
> My Tippet – only Tulle –

We paused before a House that seemed
A Swelling of the Ground –
The Roof was scarcely visible –
The Cornice – in the Ground –

Since then – 'tis Centuries – and yet
Feels shorter than the Day
I first surmised the Horses' Heads
Were toward Eternity –

What realities do courtesies conceal? The poem's
theatre plays at courtship and funeral (the carriage
ride will serve for both), though neither courtship nor
funeral is realized because our uncertainty about
*where he is taking me* – that is, about the whole nature
of the outing – is the purpose of the ambiguity. We are
unsettled by the discrepancy between matter and
manner. We know from the name, 'Death', that the
poem cannot genuinely be going in the way – 'kindly' –
that it affects to be going. As we proceed we are given a
heightened sense of social conventions being firmly
applied and yet drastically inappropriate. *Where is he
taking me?* Until he reveals by word or action that he is
other than the gentleman he appears the terms of the
pretence will be maintained; but the text never allows
the enormity of the truth to break out. The fatal
meaning of 'I had put away / My labor and my leisure
too' is to be inferred; it will not be declared. The poem
will instead sustain its genteel fiction that the worst
that threatens is the decorous discomfort of an evening
chill, for if the tensions which exist unspoken between
lady and gentleman in the theatre of formal manners
were ever to be spoken then they would be resolved in
confrontation. The 'Gazing Grain' is the audience
whose watching emphasizes how helplessly she is locked
in performance. In her geography of metaphysics, the
couple were going west. She should have realized (for

once, however, Emily Dickinson gives us the significance, eternity, and from other poems we infer the direction), but it is too late. The unmentionable reality, half eros, half thanatos, to which we may not politely refer, has happened. Nothing can be done about it now: that, or the realization that it was going to happen, is the tragedy of life.

Death is peripheral to the dead, if it is even that. It is not the consequence of it which dominates 'Because I could not stop' but the approach, and this is true of 'Sweet – safe – Houses' where those who are securely in the hereafter are spared death's 'affront'. If the famous 'Safe in their Alabaster Chambers' is the better poem it is because it more powerfully exposes the disjunction between life and death.

> Safe in their Alabaster Chambers –
> Untouched by Morning –
> And untouched by Noon –
> Lie the meek members of the Resurrection –
> Rafter of Satin – and Roof of Stone!
>
> Grand go the Years – in the Crescent – above them –
> Worlds scoop their Arcs –
> And Firmaments – row –
> Diadems – drop – and Doges – surrender –
> Soundless as dots – on a Disc of Snow –

In a number of attempts to find a second stanza that would meet with Sue's approval Emily Dickinson kept intact the poem's fundamental structure which is of two acts of enclosure. We never discover what the 'members' are 'Safe' from (it is not 'Nature's Temper' as in 'The Clouds their Backs together laid'). Its partner is 'Grand' and each of the two stanzas is seemingly illustrative of safety and of grandeur, but this word 'Safe' is an eroded and unattractive state for to be in danger they would need what they do not have – life. There is alabaster for them and satin for them, there is morning and noon; but it is of no significance, this grand surrounding. They lie, submissively 'meek', inert. There is something amiss that members of 'the Resurrection' have not been raised up. But the poem is written less to mock them, shut up in their solid beliefs, than to disconcert by suggesting that reality is immune to any belief.

They are without the identity of age or gender and they have no experience. We know them at an extreme of abstraction, by the discrepancy between their lot and the religious doctrine which promises to reverse it. In their eventlessness they are incapable of entering the only happenable time in the poem which is in its second stanza. Yet even there nothing changes. The wheeling and swooping of history is locked in mere motion. Diadems go on dropping, continuously; Doges go on surrendering, Worlds scooping, Firmaments rowing, just as continuously. At the place where the second stanza ought to issue into the first and life become death in 'surrender' we become locked into separate senses. As sound is invisible and sight is silent, these Doges whose *d*s dot the last two lines must be what the poem says they are. It is as futile to look for a noisy dot as it is to look for the precise, hard-edged lines of a 'Disc' in a substance as formless as enveloping snow (which Emily Dickinson used repeatedly to symbolize immortality).

The poem's last words are irrefutable but they do not consort with sense. They are discontinuous with life, yet they do occur and are lodged as a piece of pure mathematics might be. As in 'Because I could not stop for Death', the poem is an act of feigning. The pretended correspondence between experience and words does not exist because the absolute assurance and orderliness of the terms of the poems are known to be false to the situations presented in their reference. Death is no more a courteous male companion than a doge is a soundless dot and 'the Years' do not go 'above them', they go *in* them, rotting corpses, decaying stone, mouldering satin. Our sense is of artifice and discrepancy used in the service of remoteness. We are not brought home. Death is not for Emily Dickinson what it is for John Donne in 'Death be not proud': it is not a living experience. In other words, her attempt to imagine the unimaginable is grounded in the sense that to most nearly approach the real she must consciously face situations in which she is as isolated from social comfort as she can possibly be. The finest truth will be solitary.

This Puritan emphasis on the individual as the primary agent of meaning can easily re-express itself as Romanticism. We have this, too, in her poetry; but she is more concerned, not with plenitude of being, but with resilience, fortitude, self-reliance as witnessed in separateness and exclusion. There is a cluster of poems praising these qualities (e.g. # 395, # 773, # 789, # 855), of which 'The Soul selects her own Society' is representative, and they do not celebrate communion – even the limited communion of Saints. There seems to be more merit in rejecting the many than in rejoicing over 'the Society' selected, and to indicate that merit by declaring that it spurns even Emperors when it closes the valves of its attention is to betray a preoccupation with rank.

The following poem gives the basic valuation and alerts us to the way we need to reread 'Loneliness' when we meet it in these poems:

> There is another Loneliness
> That many die without –
> Not want of friend occasions it
> Or circumstance of Lot

> But nature, sometimes, sometimes thought
> And whoso it befall
> Is richer than could be revealed
> By mortal numeral – (# 1116)

That quality which makes her poetry challenging and which gives it so much of its interest, the quality of a thinking mind showing its alertness by overturning stale assumption, comes to a stop in simple assertion. The assertion is of privilege and is made unchallengeable by refusing to declare the grounds on which its 'richer' is based.

'On a Columnar Self –', she opened one poem (# 789), 'How ample to rely'. It seems to me that this was something she wanted to be true rather than actually believed to be so – a possibility to which it is always necessary to be alert in her poetry. It is one of those places where her verse becomes compensatory, for the story of her poetry and of the 'Master' letters is of a woman sometimes in turmoil, sometimes in deep joy because of a love which is anything but self-reliant. Someone genuinely self-reliant would not have been so insecure in it as to write verse defending it.

All the ambiguity of the Gothic, of thrill and revulsion, attaches to Emily Dickinson's sense of the imaginative scope of the mind, of the way it can be, as it were, dispatched on missions but also, as consciousness, go wandering in a life of its own. The lonely encounter with the self may produce the conventional apparatus of old stone Abbey, midnight meeting, clattering hooves, haunted rooms, revolvers which is presented in 'One need not be a Chamber – to be Haunted' to be dismissed as 'External' in contrast to the real 'spectre' – and the poem's ultimate thrill – which is there inside, not escaped after all. It may also produce more Puritan pieces such as 'My Soul – accused me' and 'Of Consciousness, her awful Mate'.

[56]

Both draw on the sense of an alternative self, concealed or avoided in the normal course of things but actually of vast implication. This is the doppelgänger of 'The Loneliness One dare not sound –' and 'I tried to think a lonelier Thing', and, were it not for a certain relish in these poems, it could be said to be Emily Dickinson's correlative for that hell which is otherwise as absent as sin and Satan from her work. Rooms and buildings are very important to Edgar Allan Poe's horrors which could not achieve their effect in open space, and Emily Dickinson's Gothic works in the same environment. Locked in the caves and corridors of dungeon darkness, has she got the right name for 'the Horror' in the cell with her? Or has she got the right geography of defin-ition for an insistently present name? In 'I tried to think' we end in a similar location, though the 'Haggard Comfort' (of fraternity) of those outside 'Heavenly Love' is more conclusively that afforded to the damned. The pleasurable, if desperate, vigour of the lines has more to do with breaking a taboo and crossing into the extraordinary than it has with the protracted enduring of misery.

The dogging reality of the wholly private, the incom-municably unique, is the inherited Calvinist reference point. It plays with the inconclusiveness of insecurity:

> Of Consciousness, her awful Mate
> The Soul cannot be rid –
> As easy the secreting her
> Behind the Eyes of God.
>
> The deepest hid is sighted first
> And scant to Him the Crowd –
> What triple Lenses burn upon
> The Escapade from God –

Thoughts travel. They are also, as she recognized (# 1156), not inhibited by time. So to fix Judgement at a time and place is, imaginatively, a relatively crude rendering of the teaching; and to confine Judgement to a judge, external to one's own self (secreting it 'Behind the Eyes of God') is also relatively crude. More subtly, thoughts are relentless, allowing no inner space that is not occupied. Yet the element of brilliance in this poem is that Emily Dickinson can deploy all the dramatic energies of pursuit – the fugitive seeking anonymity in the crowd, the crowd proving inadequate to give him cover, the implacable, burning anger of the chase, the inexorable certainty of detection – without relinquishing her sense that it is the mind which hunts. Moreover, in the single word 'Escapade' she shows up any seriously hoped-for escape as being as self-deceiving as a naughty childish romp with its inevitable consequence of adult punishment. The 'triple Lenses' magnify the presence of the one on the run and intensify the watching anger and, monstrously, this triple glass is as close as we shall ever get to glowering eyes.

But it is 'Consciousness' she is writing about, not conscience. What consciousness is conscious of we are not told. In that sense, like other of Emily Dickinson's poems, the poem is without substance beyond the reference of its own drama: here, an ineffectual wish to be free set against overwhelming opposition. There is judgement, but it is an expression of power, not ethics.

There is a similar question of what exactly consciousness is aware of in 'My Soul – accused me' where the position she takes up is the classic one of the Protestant conscience and once again we can see that the underlying model is not a personal but a cultural one. The Protestant conscience fears no rebuke like its own and in moral self-reliance would stand out defiantly against a whole world's condemnation. It opposed slavery, suffered for the right to combine in trade unions, went to jail for pacifism in the First World War and may be active today against nuclear weapons. Its bravery and resolution are humbling and entirely consonant with the poet's own remark to Sue that: 'To be singular under plural circumstances, is a becoming heroism –' (L 625). It ought to be wholly admirable. This is Emily Dickinson's second stanza on the Soul:

> Her favor – is the best Disdain
> Toward Artifice of Time – or Men –
> But Her Disdain – 'twere lighter bear
> A finger of Enamelled Fire –

The problem is that it risks becoming fixed in an armour of self-congratulation. It may not be able to move. 'Disdain' is not dissent, it is a conviction of superiority – of personal superiority, rather than superiority of a cause – and it is difficult to imagine 'Disdain' being a very good listener. The Protestant conscience may – as here – be more concerned with validating its own processes than with quite impersonal advances in conditions of life. The interest may be in justification.

> My Soul – accused me – And I quailed –
> As Tongues of Diamond had reviled
> All else accused me – and I smiled –
> My Soul – that Morning – was My Friend –

'Tongues of Diamond', 'Enamelled Fire': this is some way from John Bunyan. What had she done to provoke the disdain? The accusations seem to be decoratively remote from the unease and self-disappointment of an unsettled soul. They are remote, that is, from homely ordinariness, for they make a characteristic Dickinson claim on distinction.

Usually this shows in her feeling of being distinguished by suffering or by love (the two often linked). 'It would never be Common – more – I said' (# 430) gives the theme, which is connected with the wish for worth to be recognized (# 336). Honour, esteem are due. The flower is not a failed rose, but really a ravishing gentian (# 442). She could look at this distinctiveness wryly, too. The 'Chosen Child' might have a tough time (# 1021), more briar than meadow, more

> . . . the Claw of Dragon
> Than the Hand of Friend
> Guides the Little One predestined
> To the Native Land.

– But still special. Western Protestant cultures have not valued humble collaboration – to the extent that 'cooperation' often suggests willingness to accept authority rather than working together. Emily Dickinson inherited a metaphysics which privileged the Chosen and those who stand out from the crowd.

She inherited, too – and reinforced in her work – aloofness to worldly things. If we want a proper perspective on everything that supports this life we should see what fame amounts to by reflecting on the grave (# 906) 'The Admirations – and Contempts – of time – / Show justest – through an Open Tomb –'. In a poem which must reflect very badly on her opinion of her father (# 288) she mocked the very idea of worldly prominence:

> How dreary – to be – Somebody!
> How public – like a Frog –
> To tell one's name – the livelong June –
> To an admiring Bog!

and there is no contradiction between this and her sense of rank. She did not need publicity. She was above it.

That is what we have to believe if we take at face value her remarkably ferocious attack on publication

(# 709). It was 'the Auction / Of the Mind of Man', she said. Financial need might possibly justify so 'foul' a thing but, personally, she had higher standards. Thought belonged firstly to the Maker and secondly to the person who embodied it on earth. However, she had published herself and was closely associated with those engaged in the 'foul' business and her 1861 letter to Sue about 'Safe in their Alabaster Chambers', printed in 1862 – 'Could I make you and Austin – proud – sometime – a great way off – 'twould give me taller feet –' (L 238) – adds to these and other suggestions that her vehemence was fitful and consolatory. (In 1862 Higginson had put her off publication – see L 265.) In writing as she did she evidently saw publication as a matter of reputation, that is as a personal thing rather than a way of building something communal or sharing. Her poet friend from schooldays, Mrs Helen Hunt Jackson, took a robustly simple view and in 1876 told her so forthrightly:

> You are a great poet – and it is a wrong to the day you live in, that you will not sing aloud. When you are what men call dead, you will be sorry you were so stingy. (L 444a)

A misfortune, perhaps; but 'a wrong'? This makes the matter a duty.

The anti-worldliness is persistent in Emily Dickinson. The martyrs who go 'Through the strait pass of suffering' tramp through that poem's first stanza like Cromwell's Ironsides. If, as seems possible, she sent this poem to Sam Bowles as a way of telling him that she was chaste (L 251) she must have effectively suggested, too, that she was invincible and relentless. Her admired course was (# 527) 'To put this World down, like a Bundle –' for it was (# 888) 'a Drum, / Pursued of little Boys', (# 1024) 'a scanty Toy – / Bought, carried Home / To Immortality'.

She declared it gallant to fight her own battles unnoticed by the world (# 126) – but not by heaven, because she divided people (# 406) into those who wanted temporal reward and those who worked for immortality. The difference was (# 1086) the difference between 'The Things esteemed' and the 'Things that are'. 'The Fop – the Carp – the Atheist' serve 'the present moment' (# 1380) while they are all but inundated by 'The Torrents of Eternity'. The world was a place of transit (# 1202) – 'Of Strangers is the Earth the Inn' – and over all life stretched the fact of the countless precedents (# 1691):

> The overtakelessness of those
> Who have accomplished Death
> Majestic is to me beyond
> The majesties of Earth.

In her earthly life she was (# 821) 'An Emigrant' 'Away from Home' – at least, she was so fitfully for perhaps the first fifteen of the period of twenty-eight years from which her mature poetry comes, but there is a strengthening sense in her (which I describe in a later chapter) of heaven being an extension and expansion of life on earth rather than an alternative – 'to know whether we are in Heaven or on Earth is one of the most impossible of the minds decisions' (L Prose Fragment 114).

In my next chapter I move on to describe how, having occupied the imaginative space which Calvinism made available to her, she turned a battery of ironies on the more rigid and confining of its doctrines. However, amongst the ways in which she remained indebted to its thought is her radically altered sense of perspective. It made her live in comparative space and comparative time. She thinks on scales, and the gnat and the sky of her poem (# 796), the tiny and the vast, may be taken as her symbols. She was made alert to discrepancies (of which the greatest was that we are living and will be dead). Her perspective was altered by her being shown that perspective is a matter of valuation. What you see depends on what it matters to you to see. By declaring the existence of an unseen world, the religious tradition she inherited loosened the tyrannic hold of the immediate on her. It encouraged her to take further a natural tendency to be comparative.

It is common experience to feel periods when time drags and others when it flies (# 1295):

> Two Lengths has every Day –
> Its absolute extent
> And Area superior
> By Hope or Horror lent.

She reached into such experiences for insight and analogy:

> Eternity will be
> Velocity or Pause
> At Fundamental Signals
> From Fundamental Laws.

Some things gave time significance and others removed that significance (# 1184):

> The Days that we can spare
> Are those a Function die
> Or Friend or Nature – stranded then
> In our Economy
>
> Our Estimates a Scheme –
> Our Ultimates a Sham –
> We let go all of Time without
> Arithmetic of him –

If time would cease one day as far as our consciousness were concerned, it made more sense to calibrate it by such inner significances than by formal measure. (Hence

her use of 'centuries' is usually a scanting one.) This
entailed a further withdrawal from the communal since
people who were of the greatest significance for her
might have no effect on others (# 1189). 'The Face that
makes the Morning mean / Glows impotent on them –'
Space changed (# 1760):

> Elysium is as far as to
> The very nearest Room
> If in that Room a Friend await
> Felicity or Doom –

and it changed with time:

> The vastest earthly Day
> Is shrunken small
> By one Defaulting Face
> Behind a Pall – (# 1328)

Or (# 943):

> A Grave – is a restricted Breadth –
> Yet ampler than the Sun –
> And all the Seas He populates
> And Lands He looks upon
>
> To Him who on its small Repose
> Bestows a single Friend –

Emotional fact can translate without difficulty into
questions of visual perception. Size is associated with
significance but both may depend on the perceiver.
'Not "Revelation" – 'tis – that waits,' she wrote, 'But our
unfurnished eyes –' (# 685).

It is this superiority of thought to matter which
informs 'The Brain – is wider than – the Sky –' with its
conceit that sky and sea are smaller than the intelligence which grasps sky and sea as ideas. The view
which she makes use of in her fierce attack on publication, that God is the originator of thought, is at the core

of the poem's second conceit that 'The Brain is just the weight of God'. God and Brain are different forms of the same essential, 'Syllable' and 'Sound'.

The same core conceit comes in (# 327) 'Before I got my eye put out' where the superiority of insight over visual sight is given in the claim that she now sees more when blinded than she did sighted. This is joined with another idea, that total knowledge would be unendurable because it would amount to being immortal (having the all-knowing mind of God), hence being dead:

> Before I got my eye put out
> I liked as well to see –
> As other Creatures, that have Eyes
> And know no other way –
>
> But were it told to me – Today –
> That I might have the sky
> For mine – I tell you that my Heart
> Would split, for size of me –
>
> The Meadows – mine –
> The Mountains – mine –
> All Forests – Stintless Stars –
> As much of Noon as I could take
> Between my finite eyes –
>
> The Motions of the Dipping Birds –
> The Morning's Amber Road –
> For mine – to look at when I liked –
> The News would strike me dead –
>
> So safer – guess – with just my soul
> Upon the Window pane –
> Where other Creatures put their eyes –
> Incautious – of the Sun –

The 'know no other way' of the first stanza is close to 'know no better' and the closing stanza repeats this suggestion of ignorance and reckless naïvety. 'Other

Creatures' – the mass of people – do not understand the
vast forces with which they are playing. Emily Dickinson
is aware of those forces, even if she does not understand
them, and the claim to superior understanding and prox-
imity to divinity and the death – or madness – which such
divine knowledge entailed is explored in this poem:

> Much Madness is divinest Sense
> To a discerning Eye –
> Much Sense – the starkest Madness –
> 'Tis the Majority
> In this, as All, prevail –
> Assent – and you are sane –
> Demur – you're straightway dangerous
> And handled with a Chain – (# 435)

'Had we the first intimation of the Definition of Life,'
she wrote in a letter, 'the calmest of us would be
Lunatics!' (L 492) Her sense was that life was talked
about, not lived, and that people were unaware of their
circumstances. 'Most of our Moments are Moments of
Preface – "Seven Weeks" is a long life – if it is all lived –'
(L 641). Given her admiration for George Eliot, and
especially for *Middlemarch* (her other main, and even
greater, heroine was 'gigantic' Emily Brontë, L 742),
she must have rejoiced in the observation that: 'the
quickest of us walk about well wadded with stupidity'
(chap. 20). She requested: 'Pardon my sanity, Mrs
Holland, in a world *in*sane.' (L 185)

She held that (# 534) 'We see – Comparatively' from
day to day and person to person, that (# 451)

> The Outer – from the Inner
> Derives its Magnitude –
> 'Tis Duke, or Dwarf, according
> As is the Central Mood –

and that the utmost is relative (# 1291). In a sunset

she might see not an orthodox world but a sapphire farm and opal cattle and then a sea and ships (# 628), for to record what was available to sight rather than what the eye was habituated to seeing would be to record the inconstancy of experience, that, for example, another sunset was 'an Exchange of . . . World' ('It knew no lapse').

Change of scene or season, or the great change, death, intrigued her with its potential for revelation. She was often trying to catch in her poetry the moments of changeover as if truth was most to be found in the interstices of solid states. It was as if a set-change showed that, after all, the scenery for the play was only painted.

> I've known a Heaven, like a Tent –
> To wrap its shining Yards –
> Pluck up its stakes, and disappear –
> Without the sound of Boards
> Or Rip of Nail – Or Carpenter –
> But just the miles of Stare –
> That signalize a Show's Retreat –
> In North America –
>
> No Trace – no Figment of the Thing
> That dazzled, Yesterday,
> No Ring – no Marvel –
> Men, and Feats –
> Dissolved as utterly –
> As Bird's far Navigation
> Discloses just a Hue –
> A plash of Oars, a Gaiety –
> Then swallowed up, of View. (# 243)

I take 'Heaven' to be a sky and the scene to be night-fall, the onset of blackness being like the decamping of a circus. The world is temporary.

As long as it lasts, however, it is charged with

significance. The greatest legacy from Puritanism was not the vocabulary of Grace, Saints, the Elect, Justification, Redemption and so forth, or even the concepts which I have been describing above, it was the conviction, in advance of experience, that the world has meaning. Everything must matter, even if she cannot see how. 'Four trees – upon a solitary Acre' must count even if their meaning be concealed. It was not possible even to expire quietly without notice being taken ('The right to perish might be thought'). The very air is significant as an image of our future for (# 1482):

> This limitless Hyperbole
> Each one of us shall be –
> 'Tis Drama – if Hypothesis
> It be not Tragedy –

Being alive could not but be dramatic, possessed of importance beyond the comprehension of the actors who are dreamers (# 531):

> Men die – externally –
> It is a truth – of Blood –
> But we – are dying in Drama –
> And Drama – is never dead –

So Emily Dickinson, somewhat unevenly, turned her back on 'The spectre of solidities' of chance visits and random encounters, 'The card – the chance – the friend –' (# 1106), holding, at least sometimes, that she had given up life (e.g. 'When One has given up One's life'). But life has no more been given up in an Amherst garden than it has in a convent or on the streets of Boston. One of the things that shaped it in her case, besides the Romanticism which I come to later, was a caustically independent review, conducted over the years, of the very tradition which had played such a major part in shaping her mental space.

# III

# Faulting God

'I thought you didn't believe in God.'
    'I don't,' she sobbed, bursting violently into tears.
'But the God I don't believe in is a good God, a just God,
a merciful God. He's not the mean and stupid God you
make Him out to be.'

Joseph Heller, *Catch-22*, chap. 18

In one of those moments of exasperation or bewilder-
ment which come to Emily Dickinson's more open and
honest critics her biographer, Richard Sewall, quotes
from a ten-stanza bereavement poem by John Pierpont
which she copied out to send to a friend whose sister
had died. The poem is appalling (e.g. 'I cannot make
him dead! / His fair sunshiny head / Is ever bounding
round my study chair –') but she found it 'very sweet'.
Richard Sewall comments: 'One of the mysteries of
Emily Dickinson, from our point of view, is how she
could enjoy such stuff and yet write the way she did.'[1]
This is one of many mysteries of incompatibility, of
absent centres, which we encounter in her. Of course,
we live and believe amongst incompatibles. When we
consider the sporadic raids which Emily Dickinson
carried out on the gravity and small-mindedness of
religious legalism, we can sense the same absence of
strategy, the same lack of guiding purpose, of which we
are aware elsewhere in her poetry.

Remove the prior condition of reverence, and the

Bible is a very uneven collection of materials. Remove the unifying deference encouraged by place and occasion and it is difficult to believe that all the utterances which we call sermons are commending the same things to us. Varieties of intelligence, taste and sophistication are evident in religious belief and pointing out lapses in these has long been a pleasure for atheists. Were it starkly new, how, for example, could much public support be expected today for a religion which carried a gallows (the cross) as its symbol and which regularly practised a ceremony involving eating and drinking the body and blood of its founder? It must appear morbid and disgusting.

It is not the coexistence of belief and doubt or of contradiction, however, which is the problem. Nor of reverence and scoffing. We can imagine a poet who could write: 'We both fear God' (L 233), and also: 'I have just come in from Church very hot, and faded, having witnessed a couple of Baptisms, three admissions to church, a Supper of the Lord, and some other minor transactions time fails me to record.' (L 46) We can imagine a poet both revering and scoffing, but it is hard to accept that someone as capable of gravity as she was should not have brought such conflicting attitudes into dialogue.

Three biblical stories fascinated her. One of them, that of doubting Thomas who would not believe Jesus's resurrection until he had tangible evidence, I leave to a later chapter. The others are the deeply mysterious and intriguing one of Jacob wrestling with God and winning and that of Moses being allowed to look into Canaan down from Mount Nebo but refused entry to it. I have previously suggested the great influence which the Puritan legacy had on her mind. Without qualifying a word I want to set these two stories in the context of her very self-possessed mockery of the terms on which those beliefs had been handed to her. If at times –

and especially in 1862 – she went down on her knees, she did not stay there for very long. In comparison with the elusive and awesomely mysterious forces at work in life, she obviously found Puritan dogmas coarse and reductive.

They offended her self-respect. In 1858 she put on something of a display to Samuel Bowles, remarking, amongst other things designed to show her indepen- dence of mind: 'Our Pastor says we are a "Worm." How is that reconciled? "Vain – sinful Worm" is possibly of another species.' (L 193) How can we be two things at the same time, people and worms? And how can a worm be vain?

In 1864 she took her objection into a poem:

> Our little Kinsmen – after Rain
> In plenty may be seen,
> A Pink and Pulpy multitude
> The tepid Ground upon.
>
> A needless life, it seemed to me
> Until a little Bird
> As to a Hospitality
> Advanced and breakfasted.
>
> As I of He, so God of Me
> I pondered, may have judged,
> And left the little Angle Worm
> With Modesties enlarged. (# 885)

It is a poem which shows how she could move with wonderful flexibility in a number of ways from what might seem to be a single experience. Does it not derive from this (# 328)?

> A Bird came down the Walk –
> He did not know I saw –
> He bit an Angleworm in halves
> And ate the fellow, raw

*Raw!* She would not have expected the worm to be *cooked!* Before the poem has finished we are amongst 'Butterflies, off Banks of Noon', but it is 'raw' which is the original moment of startling barbarousness. It will feed her estimate of God, for he must be a predatory deity and of remarkably small mind to have created worm-people over whom he can lord it. She is plainly standing up for a 'Pink and Pulpy multitude' – as one of them. Must we not be proud of ourselves if *even God* has us for breakfast?

She found the mechanisms of religion a bizarre and small-minded fiction. Prayer, in one poem, seemed to her like a hearing-aid for God (why did he need one?):

> Prayer is the little implement
> Through which Men reach
> Where Presence – is denied them.
> They fling their Speech
>
> By means of it – in God's Ear –
> If then He hear –
> This sums the Apparatus
> Comprised in Prayer – (# 437)

Such a situation is too capricious and vulnerable to accident to command her respect.

However, the ironic assurance of that piece is only a fragment of the story. 'Of course,' she bursts out (# 376) ' – I prayed – '

> And did God Care?
> He cared as much as on the Air
> A Bird – had stamped her foot –
> And cried 'Give Me' –

A reader of the hearing-aid poem might be forgiven for supposing that she had never tried it and might be astonished to discover 'At least – to pray – is left – ' (# 502) her:

> Say, Jesus Christ of Nazareth –
> Hast thou no Arm for Me?

or the calm (# 564) 'My period had come for Prayer',
but to make a coherent pattern of ultimate acceptance
or ultimate repudiation out of these poems is difficult.
It reckons without the wariness which some of them
show or the piety of others. (# 564 finishes in wonder,
'I worshipped – did not "pray" –'.)

It is as though religious reality is concealed behind an
absurd front which does not connect with either it or
life. This is evident in # 476 where she describes planning a life of 'modest needs' and settling down to obtain
them – much as someone might prepare a shopping list.
She decides that her requirements can be met in 'A
Heaven not so large as Yours, / But large enough – for
me –' and she asks for it. For this Jehovah laughs at her,
the Cherubim get out of the way, and the earnest
'Saints' come on to enjoy the joke. She is the only one not
in on it. Her mistake was that she asked for what she
wanted and not for what was being offered. She wanted
a reality that matched her humble scale, not one extrav-
agantly out of scale, and in that was naïvely unrealistic:

> I left the Place, with all my might –
> I threw my Prayer away –
> The Quiet Ages picked it up –
> And Judgement – twinkled – too –
> That one so honest – be extant –
> It take the Tale for true –
> That 'Whatsoever Ye shall ask –
> Itself be given You' –
>
> But I, grown shrewder – scan the Skies
> With a suspicious Air –
> As Children – swindled for the first
> All Swindlers – be – infer –

[73]

Effectively this is one of a number of poems where Emily Dickinson scrutinizes the idea of heaven and has her doubts about it. Although it is a fairly robust piece of satire, it is dealing with essentially the same core of experience which far more delicate and difficult poems treat: the ways in which the profoundest matters of life do not match the received, or perhaps any, description of them.

So, even while she hurtled towards Judgement, she wondered what kind of world it was that could make something so awesome as one's eternal destiny depend on keeping in with God. It seemed sycophantic. Forget to be charming and you find yourself amongst the Damned, losing Paradise by a whisker:

> Not probable – The barest Chance –
> A smile too few – a word too much
> And far from Heaven as the Rest –
> The Soul so close on Paradise –
>
> What if the Bird from journey far –
> Confused by Sweets – as Mortals – are –
> Forget the secret of His wing
> And perish – but a Bough between –
> Oh, Groping feet –
> Oh Phantom Queen! (# 346)

It seemed that human beings had had settled on them a responsibility out of all proportion to their capabilities. A moment's inattention, a moment's distraction (we are all human), and the Queen, amongst the Elect, might not be a Queen at all.

If she had any reservations about being judge in her own case, she must have been emboldened by the contemporary, rising power of biblical scholarship. She was not isolated in looking dispassionately on the exemplary stories of other lives. The radical minister,

Theodore Parker, whom she read with surprised pleasure, observed:

> Matters have come to such a pass that even now he is
> damned an infidel, if not by implication an atheist,
> whose reverence for the Most High forbids him to
> believe that God commanded Abraham to sacrifice his
> son – a thought at which the flesh creeps with horror; to
> believe it solely on the authority of an Oriental story,
> written down nobody knows when or by whom, or for
> what purpose; which may be a poem, but cannot be the
> record of a fact, unless God is the author of confusion
> and a lie.[2]

A similar kind of objection goes, in romping rhythm,
into her

> Abraham to kill him
> Was distinctly told –
> Isaac was an Urchin –
> Abraham was old –
>
> Not a hesitation –
> Abraham complied –
> Flattered by Obeisance
> Tyranny demurred –
>
> Isaac – to his children
> Lived to tell the tale –
> Moral – with a Mastiff
> Manners may prevail. (# 1317)

Abraham a flattering sycophant, God a despot who
has to be humoured like a ill-tempered dog? The withering sarcasm of 1874 is to be found in 1863 in a poem
which contrasts the capricious indifference of a self-
absorbed Deity, casually, bureaucratically, carrying
out his pet schemes, with the appalled consciousness
which has to live out life in the schemes so arbitrarily
bestowed:

[75]

It's easy to invent a Life –
God does it – every Day –
Creation – but the Gambol
Of His Authority –

It's easy to efface it –
The thrifty Deity
Could scarce afford Eternity
To Spontaneity –

The Perished Patterns murmur –
But His Perturbless Plan
Proceed – inserting Here – a Sun –
There – leaving out a Man – (# 724)

Once again this seems to me a satirist's redaction
of the material which made her deeply anguished
work. There is a very similar structure in # 591,
except that the Sun with 'His Yellow Plan' takes
the place of God. 'Caprices of the Atmosphere' are
not allowed. There is the same self-absorption with
dignity and regulation, yet all the while in this
implacable scheme there are human beings, tiny,
explosively alive. The stars shine (# 1672), the moon
shines, the whole evening is thus arranged. My! Isn't
God 'punctual'! And the same complacent neatness
seems to me under assault in 'How happy is the little
Stone': the trouble with the so-wholly satisfactory
and adaptable object is that it is, after all, a soulless
lump: it is as if it parodies its maker: a stone is his
satisfactory expression. (The poem # 1543, a quatrain
suggesting that we get in life or the hereafter only
what we earn – a most un-Calvinist idea, and an
acerbic one – could be regarded as an extension
of it:

Obtaining but our own Extent
In whatsoever Realm –

> 'Twas Christ's own personal Expanse
> That bore him from the Tomb –)

A sense of dishonesty and double-dealing produced her most contemptuously rebellious poem of all where she seems to genuflect into the Lord's Prayer, asking forgiveness for being, sinfully, herself, but actually spurning this charade because it is God who set the whole thing up and is responsible for the 'supreme iniquity', us, in the first place. It is he who has condemned his own work and then asked for an apology from it.

> 'Heavenly Father' – take to thee
> The supreme iniquity
> Fashioned by thy candid Hand
> In a moment contraband –
> Though to trust us – seem to us
> More respectful – 'We are Dust' –
> We apologize to thee
> For thine own Duplicity – (# 1461)

This poem comes from 1879 but the attitude of defiance was not confined to an age, or a stage. In 1884 she repeated the theme: why should we say 'sorry' when we have no sense of having done wrong? Why should we apologize for our own earthly happiness just because 'heaven' feels threatened by our independence?

> Of God we ask one favor,
> That we may be forgiven –
> For what, he is presumed to know –
> The Crime, from us, is hidden –
> Immured the whole of Life
> Within a magic Prison
> We reprimand the Happiness
> That too competes with Heaven. (# 1601)

This is not the poetry which has established Emily Dickinson's reputation, nor does it suit well with that which has. It is too plain-spoken, too trenchant, when we come to it from the other-world of the originating imagination out of which she wrote her suffering or thrilled descriptions of the 'magic Prison', but she wrote it. It represents one of the qualities of her mind.

It crosses the years. In 1858, if God were 'wary' he would not allow us friends in case we forgot him (L 193) and perhaps it was then that she wrote:

> God is indeed a jealous God –
> He cannot bear to see
> That we had rather not with Him
> But with each other play. (# 1719)

But it could have come from the end of her life – and in # 1145 she said quite the opposite.

It is customary to refer to her 'Holy Ghosts in Cages' (# 184) as revealing a disconcerting freshness of vision, or her 'Burglar! Banker – Father!' reference to God (# 49) or her 'Papa above' (# 61) parody of 'Our Father' as evidence of the challenge facing the tact of her early editors, but the satirical mode is very strong in her thought. When it does not show in her tone its brisk dismissiveness may be there as a rejection of repressiveness. In # 403 she says, in a farmhouse-conversational way which binds country wisdom to biblical, that the restrictions of winter are scarcely worth observing; it is scarcely worth, that is, orienting life to the possibility of the worst:

> It's mostly, interruptions –
> My Summer – is despoiled –
> Because there was a Winter – once –
> And all the Cattle – starved –
>
> And so there was a Deluge –
> And swept the World away –
> But Ararat's a Legend – now –
> And no one credits Noah –

Is she serious or not? I suspect a modern reader looks for a wistful irony in these last lines and that the surprise is that it is not there: life should not be organized on the basis of long-gone calamities.

She scoffed at the moral earnestness which religious belief produced in a piece sent to her nephew, Gilbert (directly parodying 'the little busy bee' of Isaac Watts 'Against Idleness and Mischief' which improves 'each shining hour'), to which she appended the title 'The Bumble Bee's Religion' and which 'is said to have been accompanied by a dead bee' (*Poems*, p. 1050). The bee, with its dirgelike drone, works itself to death and involuntarily demonstrates to a lilac the futility

> Of Industry and Morals
> And every righteous thing

for the lilac does absolutely nothing but idle around in 'the divine Perdition' of spring. If that (happiness on earth) is what damnation is, we must surely prefer it (# 1522).

In 1869 she found a contradiction in being offered the consolation of forgiveness and love only to have that offer abruptly withdrawn if it had not been accepted by cut-off date at death. Such a religion which had not the confidence to take love beyond the grave must surely basically doubt itself, for all its fervent declarations:

> Ourselves we do inter with sweet derision.
> The channel of the dust who once achieves
> Invalidates the balm of that religion
> That doubts as fervently as it believes. (# 1144)

Probably in 1881 she was using similar vocabulary in a note at the foot of her happy stone poem: 'Heaven the Balm of a surly Technicality!' Whatever the exact reasoning (her editor believes it to be 'a reflection on

[79]

the Calvinist orthodoxy that only the "saved" get into heaven'), her general objection is to the apparently arbitrary setting of terms and conditions which make so much of the death of the body.

In 1873 she put the same challenge again: why did healing have to stop at death? And she added another: how could she be held to be in debt to heaven when she was not party to the original contract? (# 1270) This last point she repeats in an undated prose fragment:

> We said she said Lord Jesus – receive my Spirit – We were put in separate rooms to expiate our temerity and thought how hateful Jesus must be to get us into trouble when we had done nothing but Crucify him and that before we were born – (L Prose Fragment 51)

Once unlock the habit of unthinking deference, once begin to be intelligent, and the contracted perspectives of a timorous morality seem inadequate to life. Are little children really punished by the mighty Deity for mere naughtiness?

> So I pull my Stockings off
> Wading in the Water
> For the Disobedience' Sake.

Is life capable of regulation? Can it be lived for 'ought to'?

> Boy that lived for 'or'ter'
>
> Went to Heaven perhaps at Death
> And perhaps he didn't
> Moses wasn't fairly used –
> Ananias wasn't – (# 1201)

The enormities of Calvinism, like the grandnesses of heaven, do not seem to address the inconsequential littlenesses of life (so she prays in # 61 that her 'Papa above' will reserve a place for the nibbling rat while

the gigantic metaphysical apparatus of time revolves
away – much as in 'Safe in their Alabaster Chambers').
The reductions of Calvinism do not seem to acknowl-
edge life's scope. So she is required to see herself as a
naughty child who must conform if she is to be accepted – and who may not be accepted in any case. She
had experimented – awkwardly – with that view herself (# 70) and modified it and then modified again and
again until she felt awkward at having adjusted it so
often (# 1258).

With the levity which characterizes such protests
she objects (# 1545) to the mystification and dis-
honesties and picture-book simplifications of the Bible,
objects most to its resting on the coercions of external
authority rather than intrinsic interest; and objects,
late in life, to Calvinist division:

> Boys that 'believe' are very lonesome –
> Other Boys are 'lost' –
> Had but the Tale a warbling Teller –
> All the Boys would come –
> Orpheus' Sermon captivated –
> It did not condemn.

This is of a piece with the acerbic note which she wrote
at the foot of 'The Bumble Bee's Religion', setting –
probably unfairly – the New England enthusiast
Jonathan Edwards (who was at the heart of the Great
Awakening of the 1740s) in opposition to Christ. Edwards
had attempted to rekindle love and wonder in Calvinism without relinquishing its warnings of dire punishment. She seems to have noticed only the latter:

> 'All Liars shall have their part' –
> Jonathan Edwards –
> 'And let him that is athirst come' –
> Jesus – (L 712)

Mere witticisms to amuse her nephews (one aged six,

the other twenty-one)? No; they say something substantial about her. In her second letter to T. W. Higginson she wrote about her family and included the remark: 'They are religious – except me – and address an Eclipse, every morning – whom they call their "Father".' She is putting on a performance, but the nature of that performance is interesting as showing what she wanted to break from.

When she talked flippantly about Moses (# 597) she was talking seriously about herself and it gives her basic orientation, but we should be mistaken to suppose it her only message.

> It always felt to me – a wrong
> To that Old Moses – done –
> To let him see – the Canaan –
> Without the entering –
>
> And tho' in soberer moments –
> No Moses there can be
> I'm satisfied – the Romance
> In point of injury –
>
> Surpasses sharper stated –
> Of Stephen – or of Paul –
> For these – were only put to death –
> While God's adroiter will
>
> On Moses – seemed to fasten
> With tantalizing Play
> As Boy – should deal with lesser Boy –
> To prove ability.

She closes the poem with further observations on the justice of the case, but the core of the grievance has been given: to tantalize, to let him see but not take possession, to hold out a possibility but deny fulfilment. It is a fundamental structure in Emily Dickinson's work: to want and be denied, to reach out but not to hold. And it operates as an image of mortal life in its stance towards immortality. Its reverse side is to disparage what you do hold – and such disparagement is wholly characteristic of that Puritanism which mistrusts the senses, which must always be moving on because something better has been promised, which will not stop and relish. When she is enjoying herself at the expense of the stiffness and narrowness, the human incompleteness, of received religious instruction, her light-heartedness is engaging and effective, but she is perfectly capable of producing her own brand of restraints and austerities in the name of the ideal.

Remarkably, the temperamental reluctance to be satisfied becomes, when it is codified in aphoristic verse, a cramping doctrine itself. Wearingly, she gnaws at contentment. Again and again, she tells us that the value of something lies in not having it. 'Success is counted sweetest / By those who ne'er succeed' (# 67), 'My Portion is Defeat' (# 639). A gem is better *not* displayed but kept out of sight (# 1108); a riddle is better not solved (# 1417, # 1222); ownership is less to be valued than deprivation (# 801); a relation better unconsummated than not (# 213); a face more intriguing veiled than revealed (# 421); uncertainty better than knowledge (# 1331, # 1413); but, more than anything else, a feast is better not eaten (# 579, # 1240). Why so? Well, privation sharpens the appetite. The food is more valued (# 994). Eating is actually a disappointment (# 439). Satisfaction is suspect (# 1036). (It is in this general context that I think we should read her poem 'As the Starved Maelstrom laps the Navies'.) She is good at finding reasons and she says the same type of thing so often that we become suspicious of her need to say it, but I do not think that she is in the position of the fox celebrating frustration by speculating that fulfilment must be sour. It is rather that it is evasive to treasure the pangs of hunger because it inhibits full confrontation with the challenging and bewildering range of life that opens when the mind is taken off the stomach (I make use of her food metaphor). She does not always distinguish between, on the one hand, clear-eyed awareness that there is more to life than the satisfaction of the moment (however deep) and, on the other, truncation of experience, or even frightened flight from it. Whatever what might be called her precepts may have produced in her life, they did not produce the creative effort that went into lines on the hummingbird, the snake, the spider, the mushroom. The difference between those poems which advocate seeking nutriment from frustration and the references to the Moses story which briskly censure it as an injustice is a difference between the ardent and the droll, between submission to the psychology of Puritanism and breezy, witty liberation from it.

We encounter a previously noted pattern: the tradition had captured her imagination but not her assent. So her satirical pieces pick out that culture where it breaks down, without offering replacements. Her sense is of the tradition's inadequacies but she still needs its supports.

Wrestling with God is a paradigm of this process. In # 865 she describes someone (herself disguised as 'He'? her lover?) as defeating Time, the Stars and Sun, and finally as challenging God in combat. The wrestling-ring is in effect a nimbus of light which she sees as a fitting arena for the challenger. It comes, of course, from God, 'The larger Glory for the less', but there is no end to that bout. What a predicament humanity is in if, instead of being thwarted as Moses, the positions are reversed and it is victorious as Jacob:

> A little East of Jordan,
> Evangelists record,

[84]

A Gymnast and an Angel
Did wrestle long and hard –

Till morning touching mountain –
And Jacob, waxing strong,
The Angel begged permission
To Breakfast – to return –

Not so, said cunning Jacob!
'I will not let thee go
Except thou bless me' – Stranger!
The which acceded to –

Light swung the silver fleeces
'Peniel' Hills beyond,
And the bewildered Gymnast
Found he had worsted God! (# 59)

The tone at the close is almost that of Dickens's Joe
Gargery: 'Wot larks!' – you are not supposed to win
against God. It leaves questions about what to do next.

Emily Dickinson repeatedly asked them – she is an
expert with the trailing question, the reverberating
subjunctive. Although the natural thing to do is to
follow the contours of her explicit thought and make
death the watershed, she may actually be said to have
left the world she knew in other dimensions than that
for which death is the allegory:

The going from a world we know
To one a wonder still
Is like the child's adversity
Whose vista is a hill,

Behind the hill is sorcery
And everything unknown,
But will the secret compensate
For climbing it alone? (# 1603)

# IV

## Nicodemus' Mystery

> All this and more I cannot tell –
> A furtive look you know as well –
> And Nicodemus' Mystery
> Receives its annual reply! (# 140)

Nicodemus had trouble with figures of speech. In what
now seems a bemused and almost wilfully obtuse display of literal-mindedness (John 3:4), he saw birth and
death as only biological matters. It escaped him that
the real mystery was not in being born and dying
(starting and stopping) but in coming to consciousness.
Not merely being alive but knowing that you are alive,
not eating but being able to think about eating, having
thoughts which can be sent – or will wander – outside
the immediate moment: this is the mystery. It is not
one to be resolved by the biochemical analysis of mechanism, or by the production of artificial intelligence in
machines which will *do* but which do not *know* even
their own doing (syntax is not semantics, in John
Searle's phrase).[1] Nor is the mystery of consciousness to
be resolved by pointing out that its content and its
processes are powerfully shaped by historical circumstances. It can initiate change; it is not determined.
When Christ offered Nicodemus a transfiguration of
consciousness that he called being born again and
seeing the kingdom of God, Nicodemus misinterpreted
because he had never appreciated what it was that was

[86]

to be transfigured. He could think only physically.

His difficulty was connected with the discrepancy between consciousness and life. Given sustenance, the body's pumps will go on pumping and its valves will go on opening and closing until the body fails. It is to this largely involuntary body-life that consciousness finds itself attached – attached, but not the same because, for example, consciousness may be eclipsed in sleep when the body-life continues. Forms of words make use of this discrepancy between an automatic body-life and consciousness – 'Life ought to be lived', 'I've had a happy life', 'What's life for?' – and Emily Dickinson's poetry frequently requires us to be alert to it. We may say that, even while we think about it, life is moving us on as a conveyor-belt, or that life is uncoiling itself like rope or ribbon. For her part, she sometimes (as in the poem 'That love is all there is') saw life as a carrier (e.g. 'groove') which conveys or supports meaning (e.g. 'freight'). She frequently refers to this difference between life and consciousness, but this may be obscured by her conviction that body-life is itself the expression of a meaning ('love') and not just a matter of pumps and valves.

To avoid making Nicodemus' mistake of muddling up Rabbinic discourse with old men and wombs it will help to remember that her attention is taken up by the life of inner meanings. It will also help in this to recall a comparison of hers. She liked to see a life as a seed (e.g. # 1047). Bodily existence is thus the 'capsule' (# 998, # 1264) or 'rind' (# 511) which carries the mysterious 'germ' of life (# 998). This thoroughly Romantic, organic theory ought to have meant that she had a sublime confidence in the unfolding of life – provided nothing interfered with the natural process. But it rarely does mean that, and it did not in her case.

It would have been unlike Emily Dickinson to have been settled and secure in her belief, and, in a way that

is confusing at first, she oscillated between the view
that insight is given as naturally as a flower grows from
seed and the rival view that it comes from experience.
On the one hand she said that she had never seen moor
or sea but, just as she knew what they were like, so, too,
she was confident of heaven as if the tickets ('checks')
had been issued (# 1052):

> I never spoke with God
> Nor visited in Heaven
> Yet certain am I of the spot
> As if the Checks were given –

On the other hand she could say that (# 1018): 'Who saw
no Sunrise cannot say / The Countenance 'twould be'
and that (# 1241) sunset is a revelation which you see
and not one which could be imagined. Moreover, in a
similar vein, she could recall (# 1498) a memory of an
icy road with boys sledging and (presumably looking at
the same road again – though the very occurrence of
memory alone would be sufficient for the deduction)
observe: 'It is the Past's supreme italic / Makes this
Present mean –'. Her sense of the present has been built
up out of experience. However, she was transmitting
her sense of life and not lecturing in epistemology and it
is important not to have too limited a conception of what
experience might mean. T. S. Eliot famously made the
same point: 'A thought to Donne was an experience; it
modified his sensibility.'[2] A thought was an experience
to Emily Dickinson, too, and (# 1241) she did not want
to impede or falsify it by making it fit:

> let not Revelation
> By theses be detained.

To pursue the comparison with a flower, memory of an
experience might actually be part of the flower's unfolding. More important than checking the poetry for
consistency is to recognize the Romantic orientation

which guides the thought, even when it expresses itself in unRomantic language:

> Experiment escorts us last —
> His pungent company
> Will not allow an Axiom
> An Opportunity.

We do not know what the final experience, death, will bring – she is saying – so we cannot establish doctrines because they may not take account of this experience. This view, however, has its origins as much in a feeling about life as in her eschatology.

She distinguished life from belief and life from words and persistently preferred life. She evidently felt that there was some raw life-stuff untouched by belief and untouched by language and to which she should be faithful. In her view it would be a mistake to try to codify it because then the life-stuff would have been falsified. So she is constantly wary of 'terms' but also of beliefs inasmuch as beliefs represent rationalizations of the mysteries of life. They are seen as secondary (# 97):

> The rainbow never tells me
> That gust and storm are by,
> Yet is she more convincing
> Than Philosophy.

It is the life-stuff which enables philosophy to have any meaning.

'Terms' (words) falsify. Eloquence is wordless (# 1268) and we do not gain knowledge by language (# 420): 'By intuition, Mightiest Things / Assert themselves – and not by terms –' so it is as idle to ask for reasons for love (# 480) as to ask the grass for reasons when the wind blows and (# 1472) 'True Poems flee'. Beauty is (# 1700) 'a syllable-less Sea' which leaves the poet in wordless 'Rapture', and though we say that we have seen 'Nature'

(# 668) we are left talking about a squirrel or a bee or thunder because 'Nature is beyond description. Contrast, then, the real thing with an artist's depiction (# 606): 'How mean – to those that see – / Vandyke's Delineation / Of Nature's – Summer Day!' So, when Nicodemus puzzles over how someone can be born again, Nature does not give a reasoned, verbal response but happens, again, in spring time (# 140):

> An altered look about the hills –
> A Tyrian light the village fills –
> A wider sunrise in the morn –
> A deeper twilight on the lawn –
> A print of a vermillion foot –
> A purple finger on the slope –
> A flippant fly upon the pane –
> A spider at his trade again –

The preference of intuition or feeling to reason, the mistrust of explanation (e.g. # 812) – though, in her case, with a happy readiness to use the vocabulary of science for her own ends – the belief in prospects of Nature, the choice of solitude, the suspicion of society, the belief in organic meaning and veneration of awesome forces, are all signs in her of the workings of a Romantic inheritance. But the same legacy worked in different ways. In hers she becomes intricately involved in the question of what we know.

If we are dealing with a unity, what we know and we who know will tend to converge. If the whole meaning of life is love, how can we know anything but love? The carrier and the thing carried are indistinguishable. Knowledge is something lived. It is not secondary.

We see this again in (# 988):

> The Definition of Beauty is
> That Definition is none –
> Of Heaven, easing Analysis,
> Since Heaven and He are one.

She claims that the words 'beauty' and 'heaven' exactly match each other. There is no overlap. (Reverting to the Calvinist model which I described earlier, we can see that, in God's perspective, language would cease to be necessary because all words would be synonyms for God and not separate labels for parts of humanly fragmented experience. Some such sense I take to have informed Emily Dickinson's reference to 'a syllable-less Sea'.)

This imposition of language on experience is clear enough to see as long as we are dealing with something seemingly external such as flowers. It becomes more intricate to follow when the experience on which abstract language is being imposed is itself abstract. I take the flowers first:

> The Veins of other Flowers
> The Scarlet Flowers are
> Till Nature leisure has for Terms
> As 'Branch,' and 'Jugular.'
>
> We pass, and she abides.
> We conjugate Her Skill
> While She creates and federates
> Without a syllable. (# 811)

Nature creates. We name. However, what has been lost in the naming has been the suggestion of 'other Flowers', of a larger pattern of meaning in which these flowers take their place.

In our lives what might be lost is a larger pattern of Life, however we characterize that pattern. D. H. Lawrence pressed this acknowledgement on Tom Brangwen in *The Rainbow* when 'he knew that he did not belong to himself'. Emily Dickinson was constantly exploring what she belonged to, and it is this investigation which startles because it does not accept the

[91]

easy slippages on which comfortable, everyday speech depends. So life meaning 'respiration' is kept distinct from life meaning 'identity' in her: 'The first Day that I was a Life.' (# 902)

If belief were simply a matter of accepting a satisfactory blueprint for life, it would be like declaring, as she wittily does (# 1405), that bees do not live in a haphazard world but in a universe that is purposefully planned and whose plan therefore makes it invulnerable to accident – the bees' pollen is 'Fuzz ordained – not Fuzz contingent'. But belief is searing. Real poetry and real love would be so purely themselves that they would consume us and all the substance of Creation (in the poem, 'To pile like Thunder to its close') (# 1247). To pursue the comparison with language, it would be as if Life and Belief became synonyms whereas, in fact, words act as an obstacle or as a protection. If we fully understood the implications of a word (in the poem, 'Could mortal lip divine'), mortal life would be destroyed by the knowledge; and it is this sense of hers that knowledge is recognition (and thereby a revelation of life's enormous power) which she brings to her interpretation of the Old Testament idea that no one could see God and survive. It is of the very essence of human awe, she says (# 1733) that it skirts the edges of the familiar – as if we knew the house of awe but never went inside it. It stops our understanding and threatens life: 'A grasp on comprehension laid / Detained vitality.' (This may connect with an explanation for isolating herself from friends, # 1410 – the reasons would 'ravage'.)

It is her sense of the vulnerability of the knower to the knowledge (as in the poem, 'I stepped from Plank to Plank') that gives her 'that precarious Gait / Some call Experience', and the following poem shows how she uses a disruption (death) of the smooth continuum of

[92]

existence to make her mind confront once more the possibilities latent in life:

> I never hear that one is dead
> Without the chance of Life
> Afresh annihilating me
> That mightiest Belief,
>
> Too mighty for the Daily mind
> That tilling its abyss,
> Had Madness, had it once or twice
> The yawning Consciousness,
>
> Beliefs are Bandaged, like the Tongue
> When Terror were it told
> In any Tone commensurate
> Would strike us instant Dead
>
> I do not know the man so bold
> He dare in lonely Place
> That awful stranger Consciousness
> Deliberately face – (# 1323)

'The chance of Life Afresh' might well mean the resurrection of the dead, but any reference to doctrine would merely shield us from the disruption which goes on in the poem. It is not a doctrine but 'Life' which shocks – and is still shocking in the poem's last stanza. To protect itself from this 'the Daily mind' goes about its business unaware, muffled ('Bandaged') against the larger reality ('abyss') which envelops existence. 'Madness' is one name for the removal of such protection, but, in a situation which she had used elsewhere, Emily Dickinson also imagines awareness as a kind of doppelgänger whose ambush (characteristically, it is in a Romantically solitary place) existence does not usually confront.

Emily Dickinson's acknowledgements of the great capabilities of consciousness are usually of this terrifying or thrilling kind. They usually threaten to annihilate such life as she has previously known, or to break with that life, or to displace it. However, though these are the situations which are most vividly enacted in the poems, there are other verses where she seems to reassure herself by saying, for example (# 624), that God's time is like our time only unrestricted, or that (# 917) love is the basis of life, preceding birth and outlasting death and making earth actual; love (# 924) is ever-present, protectively. This reassurance is sealed in its own circuit, a faith (# 766) 'larger than the Hills', and that which shows itself in the belief that the sun is still shining in the universe even when it is not visible to the observer on earth, or that dawn will come even when it is night, or that spring will return even though it is winter. This is the kind of faith that makes the laws of natural science possible, and to attack it by observing that the sun has always risen and so always will is not to dismiss this faith but to exemplify it.

However much it may be eked out and supported by reference to the senses, such faith is not of them, as Emily Dickinson makes clear by maintaining (# 939) her confidence in a remembered image – 'What I see not, I better see' – or observing quixotically, 'I saw the sunrise on the Alps since I saw you. Travel why to Nature, when she dwells with us? Those who lift their hats shall see her, as the devout do God.' (L 321) She can envisage a life, she says (# 646), which 'may be a Bliss' and it becomes the more persuasive the more she thinks about it until it actually takes the place of what she has previously known. Such a life would not be subject to mutability, 'No numb alarm – lest Difference come' – , nor would every pleasure be threatened by the sense that it was about to end – there would be 'No Goblin – on the Bloom –'

> But Certainties of Sun –
> Midsummer – in the Mind –
> A steadfast South – upon the Soul –

This is a love poem, and it is obvious that from such happy moments came her sense that (# 677) 'To be alive – is Power –'. (It is significant that she uses this word with its connotations of will and control rather than for example, 'harmony', which occurs only once in her poetic vocabulary. Not 'power', though, but 'incapacity' is the word which comes to mind in connection with a number of the poems discussed in this book.)

The difference between mere respiration and world-changing awareness is evident, for example, in the discrepancy between human frailty, mortality and apparent insignificance and the great scale of thought which houses in that frailty. She talks of 'this tiny, insect life' being 'the portal to another' (L 39). It is that other which makes the insect life so disproportionately important. Imagining the future in a poem (# 271), she says, sarcastically:

> And then – the size of this 'small' life –
> The Sages – call it small –
> Swelled – like Horizons – in my vest
> And I sneered – softly – 'small'!

Paradise justifies her.

She is sanctioned, that is, by something which is outside history. Call it 'Bliss', call it 'magic', call it 'Witchcraft' – the change of name alters its characteristics but it does not alter the metaphysical underwriting of life. 'Witchcraft', she says (# 1708), does not have a history; it is there at birth and there at death. In wholly different vocabulary she will say that (# 1474) Beauty is a name for Infinity and we cannot be separated from this because 'power to be finite ceased / Before Identity was leased'. Beneath the images of the two poems we have a recurrence – two separate maps of the same place: of what precedes our birth and exceeds our death. (We do not think of being finite as a power, nor of identity being leased: the unfortunate effect of exegesis is to make such surprises more familiar.)

Of greater fullness than these last (which are each only four lines) is the poetry where she is not distilling life for its lessons but demonstrating the impact of what (# 618) she described as 'a Staggering Blow – / The Width of Life' which leaves the Soul stunned and merely occupying itself with journeyman labour as a way of passing time. Such a poem is # 443: what to do with life when we seem to have used it up already and yet there are 'Miles on Miles' of it still to go? Or, as she had said to Sue in 1854:

> I rise, because the sun shines, and sleep has done with me, and I brush my hair, and dress me, and wonder what I am and who has made me so, and then I wash the dishes, and anon, wash them again, and then 'tis afternoon, and Ladies call, and evening, and some members of another sex come in to spend the hour and then that day is done. And, prithee, what is Life?
> (L 172)

Later in life she might be insecure but never so lost.
Yet the passage in the letter has its poetic counterpart:

> I tie my Hat – I crease my Shawl –
> Life's little duties do – precisely –
> As the very least
> Were infinite – to me –
>
> I put new Blossoms in the Glass –
> And throw the old – away –
> I push a petal from my Gown
> That anchored there – I weigh

[96]

The time 'twill be till six o'clock
I have so much to do –
And yet – Existence – some way back –
Stopped – struck – my ticking – through –
We cannot put Ourself away
As a completed Man
Or Woman – When the Errand's done
We came to Flesh – upon –
There may be – Miles on Miles of Nought –
Of Action – sicker far –
To simulate – is stinging work –
To cover what we are
From Science – and from Surgery –
Too Telescopic Eyes
To bear on us unshaded –
For their – sake – not for Ours –
'Twould start them –
We – could tremble –
But since we got a Bomb –
And held it in our Bosom –
Nay – Hold it – it is calm –

Therefore – we do life's labor –
Though life's Reward – be done –
With scrupulous exactness –
To hold our Senses – on – (# 443)

She did not dwindle to this; she survived it. The narrative
of her life is away from it, but this is part of that narrative
and it records an actress performing the scrupulously
planned, staged movements of organized appearance
whose very triviality registers against the explicitly
declared assessments: 'As the very least / Were infinite
– to me –' but they are *not* infinite; 'I have so much to do
–' but she has so *little*. Yet the sense which denies the
words their meaning duels with another which asserts
that meaning at a maximum. Such is her state that the
trivial *is* now infinite, and that she should call this 'much'

is a mark of the great burden that presses on her now – it gives to a petal the weight of anchoring substantiality that needs a full 'push' to move it. The obligation to 'do' comes out, not of busy abundance, but of a pressure which can be resisted only by occupation, only by the purposeful allocation of 'little duties'. The poem might easily have ended at 'through' with the characteristic *this-yet-that* double movement of Emily Dickinson's thought. Had it done so, the blow would have been delivered – the striking chime for hour or quarter obliterating the ticking rhythm of the moments, but all with the orderly discipline of the mechanism. It would have been final and we should have been left wondering, as often with Emily Dickinson, how in life she had moved past the final terminal image. In fact, the poem begins again in a messier shuffling of images – errands, sickness, pain, simulation, science and surgery, a bomb and a bosom – the instability of the situation matching the untrustworthiness of judgement. 'For their – sake – not for Ours'? – it is difficult to believe her. She is involuntarily communicative by giving us scraps of other stories which do not match that polished story with which she opened. 'We – could tremble –' Why? – 'a Bomb'. Where? – inside. When? – 'held it . . . / Nay – Hold it – it is calm –' Why, then, 'tremble'? The demonstrated precision of the opening, claimed again in the 'scrupulous exactness' of the close, disappears in between in a fluster. It was a pose. The poet understood that; but, whereas she initially had sufficient composure to deploy a meticulous presence, more than the actress's shawl is slipping at the end.

A 'Reward' for an 'Errand'; a sense of completion; and a coming 'to Flesh' – as if she had been or ever would be somewhere else: these are the marks of Calvin. But it is as if there is some part of her which was not included in the Calvinist script and which finds itself still on stage but without a rationale for being there. What is unusual

– but by no means unique – about this poem is that it allows us a sight of Emily Dickinson presenting herself to the eyes of other people and sustaining herself by the fact of that observation. She has not forgotten what she looks like.

Yet the same dualism of body-life and self-life could inform quite different moods and this is evident in a poem where there is more playhouse and less drama. Life is a play but it exists in its most perfect form when it is not staged because then, after death, it takes immortal form whereas other plays disappear on performance:

> Drama's Vitallest Expression is the Common Day
> That arise and set about Us –
> Other Tragedy
>
> Perish in the Recitation –
> This – the best enact
> When the Audience is scattered
> And the Boxes shut –
>
> 'Hamlet' to Himself were Hamlet –
> Had not Shakespeare wrote –
> Though the 'Romeo' left no Record
> Of his Juliet,
>
> It were infinite enacted
> In the Human Heart –
> Only Theatre recorded
> Owner cannot shut – (# 741)

In the theatre of existence there was a Hamlet before he was ever actualized in Shakespeare's writing just as there was a potentiality we can call Romeo and another, his lover. It is as if consciousness were recovering from its own depths what originated in another place to whose size and scope it was adapted (an idea she used in, e.g., # 959). Emerson would have liked the Platonism of this but her sense of 'the best' and the hint of disdain in the

[99]

idea of a Hamlet who does not need the publicity given to him points as much to Calvin. By the characteristic Dickinsonian quip at the close the poet marks it as her own.

As script to play, as seed to flower, from infinite to finite to infinite again: this is the movement that underlies # 1047, 'The Opening and the Close / Of Being'; # 1721, with its 'Analysis as capsule seemed / To keeper of the seed'; and # 750 where 'Growth of Man' is 'like Growth of Nature' and the realization of a personal ideal (which seems indistinguishable from identity) is 'Through the solitary prowess / Of a Silent Life'. If we seek to intervene and ask for some criterion of growth that the parable figure does not provide (for how are *we* to know growth from, for example, withering?), we find the language resistant to such questioning. There is a sense of such growth either being 'difficult', effortful and taxing of patience (# 750) or else occurring quite spontaneously and without application (# 1047, # 1721). This must seem the pure mathematics of poetry, verse which takes its energies from language and returns them to language in an unbroken circuit, and there might seem to be confirmation of this in the little stanza which sees criteria as existing only when there is a deficiency (the poem, 'If What we could'). If desire and attainment were identical what would be our means of measurement? Surely we calibrate and talk about inadequacy? (For example, weather that was always totally satisfactory and always had been satisfactory would go unmentioned.)

It does indeed seem to have been Emily Dickinson's intention to make her poetry as ethereal as possible and to say this is not merely to observe that nothing rots, nothing smells and there is no sweat in her work. It is to say that she seems to have sensed that substance was an obstacle for her. The abiding realities are not earthly

realities (which obstruct access). This is what she means
by:

> To die – without the Dying
> And live – without the Life
> This is the hardest Miracle
> Propounded to Belief. (# 1017)

In this she is at her most extreme, saying that we need
to ignore all the contingencies which make our experience
– of which the physical fact of dying is one – as if there
were a kind of pure life form on which mere body-life
obtruded. ('Immortality' is a more comfortable, conventional name for it.) This is what she means, too, when
she says (# 772) that '–All is the price of All'. There is 'a
corporeal cost'. You have to abandon confidence in the
contents of life for what the very fact of life itself might
admit you to if only you could understand it. This, too, is
the thought which lies behind 'When One has given up
One's life', or when she says (# 271) that it was 'A
hallowed thing – to drop a life / Into the purple well' in
order to be admitted to a 'blameless mystery' (characteristically, in white). Such renunciation of the world – the
very renunciation that Emily Dickinson had wanted to
make in her earlier letters (e.g. L 13 & L 23) but had felt
unable to, is not unfamiliar when it is organized in an
institutionally religious way and it is not surprising
that we should meet Emily Dickinson twice (# 722,
# 918) referring to herself as a nun. However, the
identification is misleading. In her case there were no
vows. It was not a commitment, but a possibility, a self-
dramatization; and she was aware how often she contra-
dicted this idea that renouncing the world of accumulated
earth-knowledge was the way to the realest real. She
believed that the discovery of order was a projection of
the mind (# 1223) so: 'The Table is not laid without / Till
it is laid within,' because, 'Pattern is the Mind bestowed.'

How perverse, then, for the mind to actually prefer all
the casual, haphazard, random stuff that we call experience when the mind could have its own uncluttered
operations. What a paradox that the mind should violate
mind and expect experience to lead anywhere than where
the mind would have gone itself. All it was doing was
choosing instead a very crooked ('angled') road (# 910):

> Experience is the Angled Road
> Preferred against the Mind
> By – Paradox – the Mind itself –
> Presuming it to lead
>
> Quite Opposite –

It is this which explains such dicta of Emily Dickinson
as (# 1228): 'Too much of Proof affronts Belief' ('proof'
would make confidence in the realest real depend on the
vulnerable and temporary life of the senses), and as
(# 696): 'This timid life of Evidence / Keeps pleading –
"I don't know".' This, too, explains why when Christ's
doubting disciple, Thomas, appears in her poetry he is
given such unfavourable treatment. Thomas made the
mistake of trying to make faith dependent on evidence.
'Thomas' faith in Anatomy was stronger than his faith
in faith.' (L 233) Emily Dickinson treats that with
withering contempt:

> Split the Lark – and you'll find the Music –
> Bulb after Bulb, in Silver rolled –
> Scantily dealt to the Summer Morning
> Saved for your Ear when Lutes be old.
>
> Loose the Flood – you shall find it patent –
> Gush after Gush, reserved for you –
> Scarlet Experiment! Sceptic Thomas!
> Now, do you doubt that your Bird was true? (# 861)

(At the sight of a gored bird, # 1102, Emily Dickinson's
was an 'outraged mind'.)

It might seem, then, that she adopted and lived out what a philosopher would call a rigorously idealist position. However, there are complications. We have seen earlier that she mistrusted 'axioms', 'theses', and 'beliefs' because these were a codification after the fact of life. They would seem to freeze insight into doctrine. The mistrust shows in these stanzas (# 680; 'Credibility' is the damaging word she uses for the straitjacket 'belief'):

> Each Life Converges to some Centre –
> Expressed – or still –
> Exists in every Human Nature
> A Goal –
>
> Embodied scarcely to itself – it may be –
> Too fair
> For Credibility's presumption
> To mar –

A similar hostility to doctrines shows in this quotation:

> A World made penniless by that departure
> Of minor fabrics begs
> But sustenance is of the spirit
> The Gods but Dregs

If we read the syntax 'that departure / Of minor fabrics', or even if we read 'that departure' on its own, I take it that what is being referred to is the collapse of religious doctrines. They do not matter. 'Sustenance' is an inward thing. It survives without dogmas – as it were, by the inner light (an extension of Calvinism in a Quaker direction). This all seems to leave her believing in Belief as an attitude set against Experience, but not wanting to be tied down to specific beliefs. If this is confusing, the word 'trust' may make it less so. We speak of people being trusting without asking what it is they trust. (Once again the situation is one where Emily Dickinson commends something she does not have or is insecure with. She is too *busy* with experience to have the repose and acceptance that belief – or 'trust' – suggests.)

The second complication is that she could apparently directly contradict herself. So habitually does she talk in parables that, when, for example, she uses 'Life' it is not absolutely certain that she is not talking of immortal life, but, with that reservation, this seems to me to maintain that life has to be lived, not renounced:

> Between the form of Life and Life
> The difference is as big
> As Liquor at the Lip between
> And Liquor in the Jug
> The latter – excellent to keep –
> But for ecstatic need
> The corkless is superior –
> I know for I have tried (# 1101)

(This is merely her illustration of the problem. We shall see it in more substantial form in Chapter VI in Emily Dickinson's applauding heaven on earth in, for example, the experience of love between man and woman.)

Is it actually a contradiction? In logic, it is; but her habit was to take the nearest way to immortality and it is not surprising that at bleak times this should seem to her to be by wholesale renunciation and in abundantly happy times by seeking to make an article of acceptance. More significant than any question of logic in this is the consistency in the extreme nature of the hope: immortality, heaven, and nothing less, by whatever route. She held (# 1576) that: 'The Spirit lurks within the Flesh / Like Tides within the Sea / That make the Water live', and for one who felt formal beliefs an encumbrance she held it consistently; but, interestingly in the same poem, she accepted her doubt about whether 'the Adamant' – what I have called the realest real –

was in painful, difficult, trying circumstances, or whether it was to be found in exuberant happiness. 'Instinct pursues the Adamant', but when it asked for an answer to the either/or question, 'Adversity if it may be, or / Wild Prosperity', the gate of reply was closed even 'Before my Mind was sown'.

Given the dualism of life and consciousness, of flesh and spirit, what we find her doing most characteristically is not renouncing and not celebrating but exploring with fascination states which she seems uncertain whether to treat as analogues or as the real thing. 'Wonder', she said (# 1331), 'is not precisely Knowing / And not precisely Knowing not –' and such wonder is there in the poem 'A Wind that rose' where the nature of the wind is established by exclusions. (It is quite unlike, for example, the natural wind which blows through 'There came a Wind like a Bugle'.) It stirs no leaves and it is 'Beyond the Realm of Bird' for it is there to tinge a thought with certain characteristics – of the great, vast calm of polar solitariness – and to carry its movement. It has its presence in the not-world of the mind, the same place where witchcraft in Salem and Empires of Evil exist, but also where love between people is sustained, as also fear of them. The poem gives a character around which certain intangibles cohere, and we can see the same process, though more simply, when Emily Dickinson takes the story of Elijah mounting up in his chariot of fire (# 1254) and says that that chariot had no shaft ('thill') and no wheel and that the horses were wholly remarkable, too. Nonetheless Elijah takes hold on the mind – though we know it would be a mistake to ask how much he paid for hay. ('The fascinating chill that music leaves' has the same status for her – in # 1480. It shows by contrast how much we are usually subject to impediments.)

Indeed, there are experiences which some might die

without knowing. For example, there is that sense of aloneness which has nothing to do with missing a friend or with immediate circumstances, but which arises spontaneously in nature or which is sometimes brought us by thought. Whoever has it (# 1116) 'Is richer than could be revealed / By mortal numeral'. This paradox of an experience of inaccessible extents of meaning may come from memories (now beyond physical repossession) and such aroused longing is like the feeling caused by the setting sun (# 1753):

> Permitting to pursue
> But impotent to gather,
> The tranquil perfidy
> Alloys our firmer moments
> With that severest gold
> Convenient to the longing
> But otherwise withheld.

But, to put again the question of how we are to intervene in this poetry of claim and gesture, how are we to judge the verse rather than the philosophy? Can the two be separated? How can we judge the here – the poetry – when it is of the very essence of that poetry to advocate that, by whatever means, we should be somewhere else? This is a verse which is forever moving us off. How is it that we come to feel that some poems that she wrote are better than others at doing this? Inasmuch as she wrote parables, how do we come to feel that we prefer some parables to others?

I do not suggest that we should seek a comprehensive answer, but that asking the questions is helpful in exploring the nature of the work we are reading. 'This is my letter to the World,' Emily Dickinson declared in a waif-and-stray moment, 'That never wrote to Me.' It was one of her less happy claims (# 441), grandiose and self-regarding, but so resounding as to be much quoted.

By making her seem national martyr and national monument it entirely falsifies what she was actually doing – irrespective of whether or not she ever posted the so-called letter.

She was *always* writing to the world and, in the circumstances of her mind, the world was always listening to her. It was not *her* option because it was intrinsic to the fact of her using language. However much she may have deployed that shared and public potential in her own distinctive way, its very nature involves the processes of transfer and interchange. To neglect this is to suppose that the whole meaning of Emily Dickinson's poems lie in the core of what they say, to suppose that we have them once we have understood their messages. They are not transparent descriptions, however, nor are they transcripts impartially printed by someone else. She made them, and what she made thus became significant within the situations which she depicted. Obviously – to Yvor Winters' irritation[3] – she did not respect the limits which this imposed. Her 'I heard a Fly buzz – when I died' gives us a tense and person of the verb which life does not allow and I choose this illustration to help show that, in other ways too, the situations evoked in the poems give only part of the truth. In a different connection John Berger has shown[4] that paintings which use perspective always effectively incorporate a viewer though none is shown on the canvas. By a similar process we can see that no poet who declares his or her solitariness is actually alone. There is always an unidentified hearer to hear the declaration and Emily Dickinson made some acknowledgement herself that this was so by depicting many occasions where, although notionally there is only one mind, there are two presences in that mind. This lies behind 'One need not be a Chamber – to be Haunted', 'Of Consciousness, her awful Mate', and 'I tried to think a lonelier Thing' – amongst many others – and explains the apparent gibberish (# 405) of 'It might be lonelier / Without the Loneliness –'. Using words admits the existence of other people's thought – even if, seemingly, you are using those words only to talk to yourself.

By this means, paradoxically, the most private moment becomes public if it is recorded. Thus the early Puritan fondness for diaries can be seen as a calling of the conscience to public account. Emily Dickinson's is a further advance in the same line, a calling of consciousness out of its privacy and into the public world. When we recall that it is highly probable that in 1862 she wrote, remarkably, an average of one poem a day, we can see that in that year at least the poetry was her forum for life – the requirement of time needed to make verse would guarantee that.

This can be taken further. The private moment becomes public in that it becomes transmissible. This is as true of language as it is of photography. A poem is a moment waiting to be transferred to a different location and whether it is transferred or not is, like the question of whether camera film is ever developed, a separate issue. The important thing is that the mind that made the poem, like the mind that took the photograph, was not wholly and exclusively in the experience it presents. Emily Dickinson does seem to have been acutely aware of this. She protested to Higginson, in a droll way, that men and women 'talk of Hallowed things, aloud – and embarrass my Dog'. (L 271) She mistrusted the process of transmission acutely:

> A Word dropped careless on a Page
> May stimulate an eye
> When folded in perpetual seam
> The Wrinkled Maker lie

> Infection in the sentence breeds
> We may inhale Despair
> At distances of Centuries
> From the Malaria – (# 1261)

but I think that her claim that the poet (# 448) is 'Exterior – to Time' depends on just such a process of transformation and transmission. She likened making poetry to obtaining attar by crushing, and of that process (# 675) she said:

> The General Rose – decay –
> But this – in Lady's Drawer
> Make Summer – When the Lady lie
> In Ceaseless Rosemary –

My case is that the process of transmission is part of Emily Dickinson's meaning. She might declare that 'Publication is the auction of the mind of man' but she was still a prolific maker of poetry. Had she been as reclusive and solitary as some traditions – and arguably the burden of her own work – would have her, she would have been silent. Words belong as much to readers as to poets.

Paradoxically, then, these poems which urge us away from the firm and the familiar do so in terms which are a transformation of the firm and the familiar and not a negation of it. So when, in an extreme moment, she talks about 'living without the life' that is as when she said 'when I died'. Language allows it, but life does not. There, and elsewhere, hers is the poetry of experience as much as any other poet's. Poetry requires it to be so.

# V

## Of Some Strange Race

> I suppose there are depths in every Consciousness, from
> which we cannot rescue ourselves – to which none can
> go with us – which represent to us Mortally – the
> Adventure of Death – (L 555)

Some of Emily Dickinson's greatest poems are conspicuously disobedient to the laws of good sense. They
give us a world that it is comforting to call 'nightmare'
because that places it on the margins of those worlds
we know – and from nightmares we wake up. However,
I should like to withhold that word for a moment in
order to suggest that they give us a crisis of social
relation. The struggle to place and understand is a
struggle to connect with norms and such norms derive
from what is shared. The strange is a departure from
the normal.

She wrote in one poem (# 822): 'This Consciousness
that is aware / Of Neighbors and the Sun / Will be the
one aware of Death' and this may be said to have given
her the problem: how to relate the familiar, therefore
recognizable, public world with the wholly new and
isolatingly private one (here, of death): how to manage
on her own.

Outside the immediate occasions of the poems I want
to consider in this chapter, we can see her writing her
customary poems of analysis:

> Pain – has an Element of Blank –
> It cannot recollect
> When it begun – or if there were
> A time when it was not –
>
> It has no Future – but itself –
> Its Infinite contain
> Its Past – enlightened to perceive
> New Periods – of Pain. (# 650)

What we are given here is the absorption-without-limit of suffering, reconstructing the past and replicating the future, gratifying itself by denying the possibility of alternative (what Emily Dickinson called, in # 640, 'that White Sustenance – / Despair' and Gerard Manley Hopkins anathematized as 'carrion comfort').

> A doubt if it be Us
> Assists the staggering Mind
> In an extremer Anguish
> Until it footing find.
>
> An Unreality is lent,
> A merciful Mirage
> That makes the living possible
> While it suspends the lives. (# 859)

This is the reverse process; not displacement, but occlusion. The old continuum is reasserted. *That* is 'Us'. This new 'Anguish' is foreign to 'Us' and not to be believed until there is an 'Us' that stretches enough and is secure enough to include it.

But these customary poems of analysis are retrospective. They are not dramatic enactments of the kind that leave us readers asking where we start from and checking biographies of the poet to discover a cause so that we can more confidently rationalize the poetry as a mere effect. The sort of poetry I have in mind does not offer us an easy route through to our own experiences. It is abrupt and without occasion or location other than those it requires for its own seemingly hermetic processes:

> I felt a Funeral, in my Brain,
> And Mourners to and fro
> Kept treading – treading – till it seemed
> That Sense was breaking through –

She has been bereaved? No, no – there is just an idea of a sad occasion. She has been jilted? No, no. She has lost her religious faith? If explanations proliferate, it may be as an understandable human wish to be shielded from the disorder which is the very frame of the poem's setting. We like to know where we are, and wish to account for a poem whose success is to bring to us an extreme disruption.

> And when they all were seated,
> A Service, like a Drum –
> Kept beating – beating – till I thought
> My Mind was going numb –
>
> And then I heard them lift a Box
> And creak across my Soul
> With those same Boots of Lead, again,
> Then Space – began to toll,
>
> As all the Heavens were a Bell,
> And Being, but an Ear,
> And I, and Silence, some strange Race
> Wrecked, solitary, here –
>
> And then a Plank in Reason, broke,
> And I dropped down, and down –
> And hit a World, at every plunge,
> And Finished knowing – then –

There is no confident aphorism at the close. There is only an end without conclusion, and yet we do seem to have been uncannily near a procession, a service, a mourning bell and the lowering of a coffin. Such ceremonies are things we do collectively to abate the mystery of bereavement. They are formal and ordered and, in a manner, an inheritance and therefore not the product of a private volition. Their nature is to be sombre, respectful, consolatory, a demonstration, a collaboration, a salute.

In each of these stanzas, however, what should be a salute comes through as an oppression. 'Brain', 'Mind', 'Soul', 'Being', 'Reason': in each, too, there is a suffering presence of consciousness that records what is being done to it as inscrutable, only felt and heard. The poet is a unique witness, victim at her own funerary tribute. The poem enacts, as its fundamental horror, burial alive.

It is doubtful if there could be a more extreme contradiction between the self and its circumstances than to have the living treated as if they were dead but, though some of the poem's force comes from Gothic sensationalism ('creak across my Soul', 'Boots of Lead'), a weird inversion takes place and the congregation seem more insensible than the poet. They are 'Mourners', established by name rather than emotion and they tread and tread till they tread out all possibility of personal feeling. Connections are not made. There are mourners, but we are not told what they mourn. 'A Service' occurs, but seemingly independent of them. They lift 'a Box', but it is not 'my' box – nor anyone's box. Space tolls, but no one is pulling the bell-rope. A plank breaks, but again without perceived cause. This world is not accessible because, instead of being a human world of interchange, it is a world of unstoppable ritual and motion. 'To and fro', 'treading – treading', 'beating – beating': the activity (in the main, the noise expresses itself as activity rather than sound) is unrelenting. There is not a single, still moment. 'Till', 'and when', 'till', 'And then', 'again', 'Then', 'And then', 'then': the torment is the change of torments before we have adjusted to the old. The sequence goes on, unresponsive to our emotional need that we should be able to intervene to stop it.

Yet there is a regularity-order in the poem and it is of a still-recognizable, human ceremony, albeit where elements have become magnified so that again and again they impinge on the poet as varieties of heavy rhythm, indications of the irresistible process which has the plank break and which, today, it is usual to refer to familiarly as 'pressure'. Utterly a receiver, the poet uses a ceremony for the dead to define herself as a helpless victim, not of persons but of orders. She tumbles through booming space, utterly cut off from the order which exists elsewhere.

There is just such a process of orderly regulation which can be gone *through* in 'After great pain'.

> After great pain, a formal feeling comes –
> The Nerves sit ceremonious, like Tombs –
> The stiff Heart questions was it He, that bore,
> And Yesterday, or Centuries before?
>
> The Feet, mechanical, go round –
> Of Ground, or Air, or Ought –
> A Wooden way[1]
> Regardless grown,
> A Quartz contentment, like a stone –
>
> This is the Hour of Lead –
> Remembered, if outlived,
> As Freezing persons, recollect the Snow –
> First – Chill – then Stupor – then the letting go –

What more public than a funeral, or more private (it might seem) than a brain? A funeral *in* a brain muddles the two worlds, but only if we neglect the fact that funerals go on in the minds of mourners, too, as well as in places of burial. So, in this poem, there is a similar problem of alignment. There is the same sense of an order existing somewhere and of the poet being radically disconnected from it, so that instead of serving her it denies her. What more public than 'Tombs' or more private than a 'Heart'? The sense here, too, is of life being lived from the outside because the inside has nothing through which it can communicate. Here, too, there is a mechanical, repetitious tramping; here, too, a weight of lead, a numbing and a final collapse. Here, too, connections are not made. The feet go, not forward, but 'round', and they operate quite independent of environment – 'Of Ground, or Air, or Ought'. Wood, stone, lead, snow: the poet approximates herself to substance as if to claim the quality of substance that it does not feel; but this is an extreme of feeling and off the social scale. 'Yesterday, or Centuries before?' In human dimension we exist at the intersection of time and space, but such an intersection is denied when the only placement is 'after' and how long after is beside computation. 'Centuries', like 'Tombs', are long established and 'the Hour of Lead' seeks to bury this experience in precedent, just as the very first line makes a claim on the normal (implicitly, after *every* great pain this comes) but the only conquest possible in this poem is by the placing act of memory with its claim to have outlived. Even that founders because the poem will not relinquish its stubborn present tense and is indecisive about whether its experience is over and done with so that it is a celebration of survival or whether it is continuing and will be terminal. In the scene it has moved from the collective formality of being seated – as at a church service (publicly together, but concealing private turmoil) – to a personal struggle for survival in the wilderness of hostile weather. Its message which is orderly and analytic is dramatically enacted in terms which challenge that control and even threaten the message. Disciplined? Restrained? So restrained as to be frozen to death.

What is provided in 'I felt a Funeral' by the ritual of burial and in 'After great pain' by the stiff ceremonial of shock is given in 'I heard a Fly buzz' by the closest Calvinism comes to the last rites.

> I heard a Fly buzz – when I died –
> The Stillness in the Room
> Was like the Stillness in the Air –
> Between the Heavens of Storm –
>
> The Eyes around – had wrung them dry –
> And Breaths were gathering firm
> For that last Onset – when the King
> Be witnessed – in the Room –
>
> I willed my Keepsakes – Signed away
> What portion of me be
> Assignable – and then it was
> There interposed a Fly –
>
> With Blue – uncertain stumbling Buzz –
> Between the light – and me –
> And then the Windows failed – and then
> I could not see to see –

From incunabula chapbooks through to the relative sophistications of Jeremy Taylor's seventeenth-century *Holy Dying* there is a European tradition which made a good death a subject of consideration and planning, and the literature of the *ars moriendi* is a reminder that death was once a matter of community rather than medicine. It is so in this poem, but we are thrown off balance before we come to this realization because the poem poses. It says what no one convincingly can

[116]

say, since speech itself denies the claim 'I died'. So, given that the poet is not where the words are, where is she? The poem works between an imaginative extravagance that is prepared to conceive of a consciousness surviving death and a realistic severity that at once reduces that liberty to almost nothing – not flights of angels, but a single, buzzing fly. It is absurd, of course, to quantify in this way. The liberty to pass through death either is or is not there, whatever the object of perception; but the fly hardly promises self-indulgence. Although it is unusual for Emily Dickinson to pick out something that matters to her at the outset and then to set it aside until she is ready, the poem's juxtaposition of the tiny and the vast is characteristic of her.

The situation is firmly fixed in human grieving and religious expectation. The stillness in the room is immediately associated with a larger stillness and expansion of scale (as, elsewhere, 'It's such a little thing to weep – . . . /And yet – by Trades – the size of *these* / We men and women die!'). It is a critical moment: the awesome change from the things of earth to the things of heaven, the 'last Onset', then 'the King'. There could scarcely be a more controlled departure with worldly goods disposed of and all in the most cool of human orders – legal order. This is not a road-traffic death, or a death in a coma; it is the most managerially satisfactory death that could be expected, neat and tidy and waiting – until the fly.

The fly 'interposes', in that word of marvellous neutrality, between the diagram of belief, which must generalize, and the particular experience which must, in its particularity, refuse the generalization by being in some way a little different. The fly interposes between the controlling effort of deathbed ritual and the state of feeling which is other than that which that ritual allows for. Sense fading and light failing, its 'Blue –

uncertain stumbling Buzz' signifies the failure not of belief but of the knowledge which illuminates it.

It should be emerging that these poems work through processes of ceremony (which are controlling, even to an oppressive degree, but reassuring inasmuch as they provide a structure for meaning) and the subversion of such regulation which urgent personal experience brings. This is the very making process of poetry: the general, regulatory lexicon language, which both hampers yet allows, and the transfiguring press of something to be said that can find its way only through that same language. The movement of the poem 'It was not Death' might be taken as illustrating the thought of that other poem specifically about poetic inspiration, 'Shall I take thee, the Poet said.'

'It was not Death' begins with something struggled for but ungrasped. In other poems she let go, could not see, finished knowing. In this she is trying to start knowing as the means of control which is, to that extent, a means of liberation – through language, by finding the right words.

> It was not Death, for I stood up,
> And all the Dead, lie down –
> It was not Night, for all the Bells
> Put out their Tongues, for Noon.
>
> It was not Frost, for on my Flesh
> I felt Siroccos – crawl –
> Nor Fire – for just my Marble feet
> Could keep a Chancel, cool –
>
> And yet, it tasted, like them all,
> The Figures I have seen
> Set orderly, for Burial,
> Reminded me, of mine –
>
> As if my life were shaven,
> And fitted to a frame,

And could not breathe without a key,
And 'twas like Midnight, some –

When everything that ticked – has stopped –
And Space stares all around –
Or Grisly frosts – first Autumn morns,
Repeal the Beating Ground –

But, most, like Chaos – Stopless – cool –
Without a Chance, or Spar –
Or even a Report of Land –
To justify – Despair.

It was not death, but nonetheless the denied word can-
vasses a possibility that we would not otherwise have
thought of, and it sets a universal benchmark. How
minimal is the criterion of 'life'. There are fuller concep-
tions of living than merely standing up, but to apply this
one suggests the dazed condition where understanding
has, lumpenly, to be willed into action. Every rudiment-
ary step in the ponderous check is a demonstration of
the appalling depths to which shock has been experienced
and the detail of the insulting bells initiates the sense
the poem gives of being alienated from the physical
world, even when that world includes the poet's own
body. Not death, then, and not night, or cold, or heat –
none of the agreed categories, but an approach to them
as the nearest thing. However, what words will not
provide, experience outside words does. The trouble is
that the essential locating fact is a post-mortem fact.
The effort of memory to find the essential point of
connection and relatedness goes back to the dead.

The corpse in a coffin fits like a key in a keyhole or a
door in a frame – this seems to be the run of ideas, and
its terms are constraint and liberation. The tangible
physical certainty of the key – how substantial, how
real – might release her and give her space, allow her
to breathe.

In the next stanza she has it, without limit. The heart's ticking is like the 'Beating Ground' of the earth in cold, undifferentiated, unfilled space. The body which was so firm a presence in the early part of the poem, with hot winds crawling over its surface like insects, is nowhere now and the poem moves into a void. There can now be no statement even that something is wrong because the something is without feature. ('Chaos' has the orthodox sense of the absence of any form.) If we knew that there was a drifting spar we could use it to keep afloat, if we knew how far off the land was we could despair of reaching it, but we have instead a problem without configuration, a problem that cannot even state itself for diagnosis, let alone solution.

But poems are not made of such absences. What we truly have is the simulacrum of an empty sea. The poetry has an imaginative life independent of a reader's ability to put names on its causes and it has that life exactly because of the creative skill of the poet. It succeeds because of Emily Dickinson's ability to respond to the question, 'What is it like?' and, in thinking about her response, we are likely to register the intensity of the experience that required the verse. It seems to me that we deny her her experiences and the imagination its power if we maintain that these poems do not represent the world.[2] There is a seductively easy path which runs in this direction, and it begins from the observation that it is not possible to write poems about being dead. Since we have such a poem in 'I heard a Fly buzz', that poem must be a linguistic exercise. Thus – the argument implies – whatever lexical interest it may have for us, it is of no use to our emotional and spiritual lives. It cannot educate us. (In similar vein, philosophy used to exercise itself about what to do with the sentence,

'The King of France has a beard', when France is a country without a king.) But this approach is mistaken because the imagination will not be constrained. It is impossible, for example, for Death to be not proud because the cessation of life cannot be proud, humble, impertinent, or anything at all. It is impossible for Pity like a naked, new-born babe to bestride the blast because naked new-born babies do not bestride anything (never mind the blast – which, in their case, would be terminal). It is impossible for the Blessed Damozel to lean out of Heaven because heaven has not the solidity to support such nonchalance. The imagination deals in impossibilities. The hard thing is to relate these impossibilities to the possible.

In seeking such relation in Emily Dickinson's case we can remark the fertility of the imagination which, though it employed a common idiom, structured so many varied situations. Death, numbness, falling, oppressive solidity, weight, imminent catastrophe, utter motionlessness, highly organized rituals or patterns which have no human sense and are enclosed in their meanings, passivity amongst staring or amongst hectic activity, imprisonment which may be both protective and disabling, the absence of spatial or temporal unity: hostility and disjunction are the terminology of this world. It is no surprise to know that there is not a kind smile in it anywhere.

Yet this world is not a uniform one. Within it there are degrees of collapse and recuperation. 'A Clock stopped' is secure in its abandonment of hope and, in contrast, it is poems such as 'That after Horror' or 'The Soul has Bandaged moments' which because they are dynamic may also present situations more frightening.

> A Clock stopped –
> Not the Mantel's –
> Geneva's farthest skill

Can't put the puppet bowing –
That just now dangled still –

An awe came on the Trinket!
The Figures hunched, with pain –
Then quivered out of Decimals –
Into Degreeless Noon –

It will not stir for Doctors –
This Pendulum of snow –
This Shopman importunes it –
While cool – concernless No –

Nods from the Gilded pointers –
Nods from the Seconds slim –
Decades of Arrogance between
The Dial life –
And Him –

We are made to reach behind the words: not a Swiss clock with its puppet, another sort of clock, unspecified. 'Figures' are numbers, and 'figures' are people; humans have fingers and so do clocks, and both have faces and both have rhythms – without working exact points of correspondence, the poem sets up an analogy which is secure outside even the explicitly-mentioned terms. But that opening sentence still leaves the reader stranded between analogy and actuality. This stranding is the state which the poem explores, the state of not being sure where you are and which, in the same line, can move therefore between the semantic extremes of 'awe' and 'trinket'. There is no difference worth emphasis, when they are stopped, between a body and a clock, but there is every difference between the clockwork mechanism and the person. Once again the poem exploits the confusion of status. 'Doctors' care for a clock, a 'Shopman importunes' a mechanism, uselessly, since mechanisms cannot respond. The coming of death is an exit from chronometry, 'out of Decimals' into serenity, cool–concernless, both fingers on the twelve, the Noon which Emily Dickinson associated, like snow, with immortality, endless and beginningless and out of measurement. But it is separation and inaccessibility which the poem ultimately dramatizes. What cannot be done and what will not be done is that the clock will not be made to go again. The actuality is now no different from the analogy.

In 'That after Horror' the security afforded by staying in one place for the duration of a poem is removed. The scene keeps changing, though generally preserving the type of unfolding continuity that comes when the imagination moves from association to association: a pier – granite; mouldering – a crumb; letting go – just holding 'by a hair'; a pier, security – water, drowning. The drama is of risk and rescue very clearly identified as matters of imaginative projection ('The very profile of the thought'). Moreover this imaginative projection is inimical to memory. Characteristically, it puts 'Recollection numb'. Why is this? It is because the orderly process whereby the poet, secure in the present, recollects some appalling feeling experienced in the past – and recollects it as a means of demonstrating control over that feeling – is jeopardized by the very thing recollected. There is a politics of memory. Memory may be a victory celebration. Here, however, it is a defeat. With the instant speed of the imagination, the past may become the present. The past may be the future, grotesquely staring us mockingly in the face in an image which, as David Porter says,[3] reminds us of Epstein's 'Rock Drill':

> The possibility – to pass
> Without a Moment's Bell –
> Into Conjecture's presence –
> Is like a Face of Steel –
> That suddenly looks into ours
> With a metallic grin –

The Cordiality of Death —
Who drills his Welcome in —

This is not 'after Horror', it *is* horror; a feared image of
'us', mocked, threatened and alienated.

This substitution of a funeral-world, a coffin-world, a
clock- and drill-world for a responsive and feeling world
of human communication is evident in 'The Soul has
Bandaged moments' where there is a similar element
of mimicry and caricature that takes human characteristics and denatures them. Here is not a ferocious
'cordiality' but an Aubrey Beardsley-like decadent
which supplants the place of love and does what love
would do — except that it is in hideous parody of it. The
'Goblin' comes unbidden and the soul feels ashamed to
be thinking such a thing; but the 'thought' — the
imagined horror — is there as one of the mind's possibilities.

> The Soul has Bandaged moments —
> When too appalled to stir —
> She feels some ghastly Fright come up
> And stop to look at her —
>
> Salute her — with long fingers —
> Caress her freezing hair —
> Sip, Goblin, from the very lips
> The Lover — hovered — o'er —
> Unworthy, that a thought so mean
> Accost a Theme — so — fair —

But the mind can, temporarily, rid itself of such beset-
ting horrors. As in # 1128, like a winged insect with
the freedom of the air, it is liberated, dying into immortality ('Noon' again — the vocabulary is constant).
The paralysis, imaged by the self-protective, restraining bandages, is shown to have been a dreadful
denial of the self's real nature:

[124]

The soul has moments of Escape –
When bursting all the doors –
She dances like a Bomb, abroad,
And swings upon the Hours,

As do the Bee – delirious borne –
Long Dungeoned from his Rose –
Touch Liberty – then know no more,
But Noon, and Paradise –

If we seek the reassurance of paraphrase we could say
that Emily Dickinson had been so miserable that she
had wanted to die, but this crudely reductive account
would falsify the verse. Death would not be a termination,
it would be a release and a fulfilment, the reaching of
the 'Rose'. But that is only one of a range of futures:

The Soul's retaken moments –
When, Felon led along,
With shackles on the plumed feet,
And staples, in the Song,

The Horror welcomes her, again,
These, are not brayed of Tongue –

It is like being recaptured. It is like being free to choose
where to go one moment and being 'led' the next, like
being able to fly and being shackled, like being song
returned to a cacophonous, braying mockery of welcome.
It is like having feelings transferred from 'The Soul
has Bandaged moments' to ''Twas like a Maelstrom,
with a notch'.

Just as Emily Dickinson seems to have thought of a
bomb in the same connection as an insect bouncing and
droning across a ceiling (# 1128), she seems to have
thought of a notch in the same connection as a mark on
the whites of spinning wheels where they have passed
through floods (# 788). The poem has a number of such

exact markers which scrupulously calibrate only how near or how far we are from the disaster which, just as it is about to arrive, is always replaced by a new version of approaching calamity. Nearer, nearer, the maelstrom brings 'its boiling Wheel', toying – as the sipping Goblin might have done, 'with the final inch'. Then something broke (something comparable to a plank in reason?) and the tormented subject is released just as surely as at the close of 'I heard a Fly buzz' or 'After great pain', but in this poem the fascinating measure is back. Not the numerals of the exact clock face, nor the predetermined patterns of the funeral service or the 'Hour of Lead', but:

> As if a Goblin with a Gauge –
> Kept measuring the Hours –
> Until you felt your Second
> Weigh, helpless, in his Paws –
>
> And not a Sinew – stirred – could help,
> And sense was setting numb –
> When God – remembered – and the Fiend
> Let go, then, Overcome –

Just as helpless as in 'I heard a Fly buzz' or 'After great pain' or 'I felt a Funeral', just as numb, just as oppressed by heavy time, the poet can do nothing. Then the universe snaps haphazardly into memory and the poet, toyed with by this process as surely as by the sipping Goblin, is rescued – only to be at risk again a moment later:

> As if your Sentence stood – pronounced –
> And you were frozen led
> From Dungeon's luxury of Doubt
> To Gibbets, and the Dead –

> And when the Film had stitched your eyes
> A Creature gasped 'Reprieve'!
> Which Anguish was the utterest – then –
> To perish, or to live?

In the absolute certainty of death there seems at last a fixture, then the fixture is removed. Has not 'reprieve' subverted its own meaning?

In however manic a context, measure is relatedness, and in # 561 we see Emily Dickinson doing more straightforwardly what emerges in the Maelstrom poem in such contortions. The straightforwardness comes from her having the initiative. It is not that she is measured, now she does the measuring – socially, comparatively:

> I measure every Grief I meet
> With narrow, probing, Eyes –
> I wonder if It weighs like Mine –
> Or has an Easier size.

Some, she presumes, 'are like My Own'.

There is an engaging poem (# 576) in which she describes praying as a little girl because she had been told to pray and later stopping when she had sufficient imagination to think what it must be like to be on the receiving end of one of her ensuing shopping lists to God. If only she now had such a God as the one of her girlish requests he would steady her life for her till she could take the balance herself. As it is, 'It takes me all the while to poise – / And then – it doesn't stay –'.

It is easier to balance if the world is not moving. The distinctive feature of most of the poems discussed above is that the world does move. Pain is more real than matter, 'so utter – / It swallows substance up' ('There is a pain') and determines its own topography. The terms are ones of claustrophobic confinement or self-annihilating emancipation. 'I felt the Columns close', she writes in the poem which opens 'I saw no Way', but when, at the merest touch, the whole scene changes, 'I alone – / A Speck upon a Ball – / Went out upon Circumference'. Beyond the arc of a bell's swing, out of scope, out of meaning, the poet goes past the perimeter of the known.

In an earlier chapter I suggested that the effect of the preaching she listened to would have been to remove the security of the substantial world. Confronted with a crisis in her inner life we can well see that she might lose what Alan Ross has called 'the casual knack of living' and believe, for a time (# 928):

> That Calm is but a Wall
> Of unattempted Gauze
> An instant's Push demolishes
> A Questioning – dissolves.

Calm, in other words, is inexperience. Test it and it will fail. The hair that secures in 'That after Horror' is all that stands between precarious life and the enormous totality of Eternity ('Crisis is a Hair').

Without some confidence in a continuum of experience life cannot be lived but only maintained from outside by the operations of other people. At some time, probably in 1862, in the process of recovery, Emily Dickinson faced the possibility that her identity was in doubt:

> The first Day's Night had come –
> And grateful that a thing
> So terrible – had been endured –
> I told my Soul to sing –
>
> She said her Strings were snapt –
> Her Bow – to Atoms blown –
> And so to mend her – gave me work
> Until another Morn –

And then – a Day as huge
As Yesterdays in pairs,
Unrolled its horror in my face –
Until it blocked my eyes –

My Brain – begun to laugh –
I mumbled – like a fool –
And tho' 'tis Years ago – that Day –
My Brain keeps giggling – still.

And Something's odd – within –
That person that I was –
And this One – do not feel the same –
Could it be Madness – this? (# 410)

However, against the tenor of the poem's closing
question, the mere allocation of a social name is a
victory and the mere act of placement in a secure
memory is also a victory. So she describes (# 590)
being 'in a Cavern's Mouth –/ Widths out of the Sun' on
her own – 'How Goblin it would be –' or looking into the
yellow eye of a cannon, coolly facing the question of life
and death. Has the person to whom she addresses that
poem experienced isolation in such terms? There is a
double criterion for checking the answer: 'If you remember, and were saved – / It's liker so – it seems –'. To
have been in it, and come through it. To know that you
have known it.

A cavern's mouth, a cannon's eye, consciousness being enveloped (# 396) 'As Mists – obliterate a Crag':
finding images is a means of establishing the private
as the public by relating one personal experience to
another. But, in the process, our sense of public structure is modified. The mind that links a cavern with a
cannon and a goblin with a yellow eye is making
something new out of the old and establishing new
possibilities within the range of precedent, giving us
new models for interpreting experience. In such poems

Emily Dickinson sometimes uses the strongest Christian image available to her, Calvary.

She took it, but she used it badly. She laid a claim on the name, but left it only as a name. She claimed the reputation of its pain as indicating the singularity of hers – 'Queen of Calvary', 'Empress of Calvary' (# 1072), but this is an easy traffic. She left the word smaller than when she found it. She used it for rank to index her suffering, but she paid no regard to the responsibilities that go with the shaping history. Was she really trying to claim its vicariousness? It seems unlikely.

In the poem 'One Crucifixion is recorded – only –' we see her arguing through the reduction of the word which eases her use of it in, for example, 'I dreaded that first Robin, so':

> One Crucifixion is recorded – only –
> How many be
> Is not affirmed of Mathematics –
> Or History –
>
> One Calvary – exhibited to Stranger –
> As many be
> As persons – or Peninsulas –
> Gethsemane –
>
> Is but a Province – in the Being's Centre –
> Judea –
> For Journey – or Crusade's Achieving –
> Too near –
>
> Our Lord – indeed – made Compound Witness –
> And yet –
> There's newer – nearer Crucifixion
> Than That –

History is publicity, and its selections have indeed

privileged one crucifixion above others and given it a name. So she might seem to be making the claim that Brecht makes in his poem 'Questions from a Worker who Reads', that publicized history is a history of famous names whereas the unpublished version has more to do with the collaborative efforts of great numbers of men and women who are unacknowledged. In fact she abandons history altogether. Calvary becomes illustrative of the potentialities of life, 'Gethsemane – / Is but a Province – in the Being's Centre –'. There are – in a vein of thought which is decidedly Emersonian – as many Calvaries as there are people, although an observer might be conscious only of the public Calvary, the famous one. But Calvary had a particular form, although that form might be disputed and interpretation might be a matter of fierce controversy, and that form had very much more to it than organized suffering. It had reasons. In Emily Dickinson's usage the reasons go. 'No Black bird bates his Banjo – / For passing Calvary –' she wrote (# 620). Nature is as oblivious to suffering as it is to the fall of Icarus in Auden's 'Musée des Beaux Arts'.

> I dreaded that first Robin, so,
> But He is mastered, now,
> I'm some accustomed to Him grown,
> He hurts a little, though –
>
> I thought if I could only live
> Till that first Shout got by –
> Not all Pianos in the Woods
> Had power to mangle me –
>
> I dared not meet the Daffodils –
> For fear their Yellow Gown
> Would pierce me with a fashion
> So foreign to my own –

I wished the Grass would hurry –
So – when 'twas time to see –
He'd be too tall, the tallest one
Could stretch – to look at me –

I could not bear the Bees should come,
I wished they'd stay away
In those dim countries where they go,
What word had they, for me?

They're here, though; not a creature failed –
No Blossom stayed away
In gentle deference to me –
The Queen of Calvary –

Each one salutes me, as he goes,
And I, my childish Plumes,
Lift, in bereaved acknowledgement
Of their unthinking Drums –

This is the story of someone whose world is insensitive
to her frailty. The pianos are in the woods because the
woods are conceived of as sound-making machines.
Daffodils do visually what birdsong does aurally, they
assault the senses and they refuse support. So do the
bees. The drama is of exposure and concealment. The
poet is to be stared at as a public object and she doubts
her ability to endure it. All the lines of sight focus on
her and the perspectives of the story connect the indifferent workings of nature with the fact of her presence. The world is personally significant, for so absolute
is the sensed division between her own mind and her
surroundings that her consciousness divides very
simply into 'me' and 'them'. She must be at the centre,
even though she does not wish to be. The great irony of
the closing ritual is that she, deferred to as a Queen, is
being persecuted by this attention. The salute is a
crucifixion (just as the salute of the funeral tribute in

the poem discussed earlier was burial alive). Her acknowledgement is 'bereaved' because the ceremony
might have had a wholly different significance and not
be the mockery that it is. 'The Birds declaim their
Tunes,' she wrote in another poem (# 364):

> Pronouncing every word
> Like Hammers – Did they know they fell
> Like Litanies of Lead –
>
> On here and there – a creature –
> They'd modify the Glee
> To fit some Crucifixal Clef –
> Some Key of Calvary –

It is difficult to recall adequately enough that the
woman who wrote these poems was the one who had
felt and would feel again with even greater persistence
and intensity that the mere fact of being alive was joy.
The joyfulness and the misery seem not to have tem-
pered each other, though a number of poems take
account of both extremes even if they do not open up a
discourse between them. 'I sometimes drop it, for a
Quick' is one such, its compacted opening stanzas giving way to some of the most crisp and effective images
she ever wrote:

> I sometimes drop it, for a Quick –
> The Thought to be alive –
> Anonymous Delight to know –
> And Madder – to conceive –
>
> Consoles a Woe so monstrous
> That did it tear all Day,
> Without an instant's Respite –
> 'Twould look too far – to Die –

She refused to send Higginson a photograph of herself
when he asked for one, observing of the life-mould of

herself which she had refused her father: 'I noticed the Quick wore off those things, in a few days.' (L 268) It is this sense of 'quick', meaning life or liveliness, (as in the biblical 'the quick and the dead') that we have here. Sometimes she abandons her misery for the sheer thought of being alive which is so extraordinary that you would go mad trying fully to realize it. That delight which is not attributable to specific causes (it is 'anonymous') is consolation for a misery 'so monstrous' that, if it were allowed to ravage uninterrupted, would be so all-knowing that we should never be able to put a stop to it because it would have such a grip. For this pattern she then finds analogues:

> Delirium – diverts the Wretch
> For Whom the Scaffold neighs –
> The Hammock's Motion lulls the Heads
> So close on Paradise –

> A Reef – crawled easy from the Sea
> Eats off the Brittle Line –
> The Sailor doesn't know the Stroke –
> Until He's past the Pain –

The condemned man is too delirious to be aware of his own impending execution. The motion of the hammock sways to sleep seagoers who are only a few feet above the ocean and thus so close to death and paradise that a reef can remove the brittle dividing-line between life and death. The sailor does not register that the punishment stroke has landed on his back until he has passed through its pain. She is using an idea here that we have met before in her work – in Eliot's phrase, 'Humankind / Cannot bear very much reality'. (As she put it in 'Victory comes late', 'Cherries – suit Robins – / The Eagle's Golden Breakfast strangles – Them'.) The harsh, nightmarish insistence of the gallows is brilliantly given in 'neighs' – but the neighing is not heard – and the line of life and death *is* the line of the reef, brittle to the eye where the sea nibbles at and covers it. The very range from 'scaffold' to 'paradise' suggests the great scope of the 'anonymous delight' at the same time that it advances, contrarily, the claim that that delight is oblivious to risk.

The poem is at a critical juncture between knowing and experiencing. It is wholly characteristic of Emily Dickinson in declaring the superiority of knowledge (for example, the knowledge that we are immortal though we appear to be confined in time, or, here, the knowledge that the reef threatens) over experience (for example, here, delirium, sleep, pain) but it is also characteristic of her to make this knowledge part of the experience. Why should we suppose that it is woe which looks the furthest when the beauty of her lines makes joy the encompassing fact? Is not her poetry, which knows both, a crushing of pain to distil sweetness, attar, not from the rose, but from misery? (When Elizabeth Barrett Browning died, Emily Dickinson was astonished at Browning's making another poem, 'Till I remembered that I, in my smaller way, sang off charnel steps. Every day life feels mightier, and what we have the power to be, more stupendous.' L 298)

It is as if, in such places, her meaning cried against her message. It was the contradiction in her Calvinist-Platonist preference for higher things:

> The worthlessness of Earthly things
> The Ditty is that Nature Sings –
> And then – enforces their delight
> Till Synods are inordinate – (# 1373)

That preference derived from insight into things, not repudiation of them. The poet of the next life was a poet of sunsets. Looking back, probably from nearly ten years later, on the years from which most of the poems in this chapter come, she wrote (# 1197): 'I should not

[135]

dare to be so sad / So many Years again –'. She could not believe that she had had the strength to survive. When tested, though, the fabric of her verse shows her seeking anchorage in those human ceremonies and regulators which she used to communicate her miserable isolation.

# VI

## Upon Enchanted Ground

> We dont *have* many jokes tho' *now,* it is pretty much all
> sobriety, and we do not have much poetry, father having
> made up his mind that its pretty much all *real life.* (L 65)

Emily Dickinson once wrote to Sue commending three
little books she had been reading. They were 'sweet and
true' and they will 'do one good'; and yet, she complained,
'They dont *bewitch* me any. There are no walks in the
wood – no low and earnest voices, no moonlight, nor stolen
love, but pure little lives, loving God, and their parents,
and obeying the laws of the land . . .' (L 85) What she
objected to, I think, in this picture of compliance was the
failure of those lives to inhabit larger dimensions of
being than those with which they were immediately
presented. Those little lives exactly conformed to what
Emily Dickinson might have called, had she repeated
her own, earlier, ironic phrase, 'real life'. 'Real life' for
her is obviously life misconstrued, a pitifully contracted
and dull, lumpen business, and her suggestions of what
would be preferable and bewitching give us her own
basic Romantic orientation, which in turn brings
together the present book's two major themes: her
celebration of 'a quality of loss' and her a-historicism.
    That thing of gesture, tone, atmosphere that, with
scant regard for, for example, the tough-mindedness
of Blake and Wordsworth, we commonly call 'Romantic'
*is* a-historical. What were those 'low and earnest

voices' saying? Was every night a moonlit one? When love was not being 'stolen' what happened to it on the other days of the week? The price for Romantic elevation of feeling, as it evades the constraints and awkwardnesses of life, may be contact with the real. Such feeling may be sustainable only by being continuously moved on in a series of displacements which we call 'escapism', the ultimate move of displacement being death. To some ideal heaven may be transferred all the fineness of feeling which a cruel, indifferent, stupid, or 'real' world would not countenance. Thus suicide (about which Emily Dickinson wrote two or three times) may be the supreme Romantic gesture, or the Romantic may instead live (more usually, languish) in the gap between desire and fulfilment, treasuring 'a quality of loss' as the index of the so-far-elusive higher destiny.

With its loftiness, its restiveness and tendency to fly the present world, its individualism, its longing for finer moments, its feeling of being hampered by the normal, there is a striking symmetry between some versions of Romanticism and the character of Protestant belief – so no wonder that T. E. Hulme called it 'spilt religion'.[1] The one may be seen as a translation of the other. In Emily Dickinson's position it was Ralph Waldo Emerson (like T. W. Higginson, a former Unitarian minister) who was chief translator. By using him to give the character of American Romanticism we can recognize her departures from it as well as its attractions for her.

In his version the major difference was that, whereas Calvinism thought of a heaven to come and for the few, Emerson announced a heaven now and potentially for all. Man is 'a god in ruins' ('Nature', 1836) but capable of redemption if he opens himself to the revelations not of God but of the natural world. He must not allow himself to be impeded in this by anything so artificial as history – 'We must set up the strong present tense' ('Experience') – or society, which is 'almost all custom', for the problem with the past and with books, in his view, is that, 'The sacredness which attaches to the act of creation, the act of thought, is transferred to the record' ('The American Scholar'). In his own country and his own moment, and not in tradition or in the culture of some foreign land, man might discover the paradisal truth of which he is part.

When misleading appearances and conventions have been recognized as such, 'Man is conscious of a universal soul within or behind his individual life' ('Nature', 1836). It follows that, if 'Every thing is made of one hidden stuff' ('Compensation'), antipathies are more apparent than real. So, if the open-eyed Transcendentalist builds his own world rather than accepts the social/historical one provided, 'A correspondent revolution in things will attend the influx of the spirit. So fast will disagreeable appearances, swine, spiders, snakes, pests, mad-houses, prisons, enemies, vanish; they are temporary and shall be no more seen' ('Nature', 1836).

This is nonsense. There are obviously occasions when it is prudent to keep well out of the way of one of these mere 'appearances' and Emily Dickinson's 'A narrow Fellow in the Grass' is sufficient reminder that her sense was that the natural world was distinct and different from the human. Emerson's air of serenity derives from his feeling that the world is ultimately harmonious and knowable. She had no such sense. When she opened her eyes to the real hidden beneath the daily it was to the peculiarity, awesomeness, and mystery of it, and not to let the balmy 'currents of the Universal Being circulate through me' ('Nature', 1836), as he did.

Given her own father's public life, it would be interesting to know how she placed him when she was told that 'knaves win in every political struggle', but she would not have been troubled by Emerson's complete lack of interest in reconciling that view with his complacent 'the world-spirit is a good swimmer'. His feeling that, 'Through the years and the centuries, through evil agents ... a great and beneficent tendency irresistibly streams' ('Montaigne'), is sufficient explanation for the apparent contradiction; it left the matter out of man's hands and history quite pointless.

She would have been pleased, too, by Emerson's idea that the true aristocrat (for a daughter of the republic how many favouring references to feudal rank there are in her poems) could be perfectly content with his own mind, whereas the common man (the many) allowed himself to be the victim of events. We can see the mark of Calvin in this, but it would be the anti-Calvinist in her which warmed to the idea that: 'The soul knows no persons. It invites every man to expand to the full circle of the universe' ('Divinity School Address').

It can well be seen how popular such a stance might be for an emergent nation with a sense that its own past was very short (Europe's, in contrast, being very long) but that its own, only partly explored, territory was vast. Emerson effectively substituted geography for history. In the metaphysics of her poetry Emily Dickinson did the same. She gave the spirit a landscape rather than a past and thus the stay-at-home put herself in tune with a national mood.

The two faced the same way, even if they looked with different eyes. Thus Emerson writes, characterizing the resistance of orthodoxy in a way that her radical intelligence must have approved:

> For it is the inert effort of each thought, having formed itself into a circular wave of circumstance, – as for instance an empire, rules of an art, a local usage, a religious rite, – to heap itself on that ridge and to

solidify and hem in the life. But if the soul is quick and strong it bursts over that boundary on all sides and expands another orbit on the great deep . . .

. . . There is no outside, no inclosing wall, no circumference to us. ('Circles')

For her, of course, there was a circumference, but she lived in the same essential metaphor, operating at the edges of the familiar. The alignment of sympathies is made clear by Emerson's distinction between idealists and materialists. The idealist thinks the world an appearance:

The materialist respects sensible masses [i.e. material bodies], Society, Government, social art and luxury, every establishment, every mass, whether majority of numbers, or extent of space, or amount of objects, every social action. The idealist has another measure, which is metaphysical, namely the *rank* which things themselves take in his consciousness; not at all the size or appearance . . . ('The Transcendentalist')

Poets, he thought, were 'liberating gods'; 'They are free, and they make free' ('The Poet').

It is not surprising, therefore, that it was after Emerson had stayed next door in 1857 that Emily Dickinson is believed to have written her remark: 'It must have been as if he had come from where dreams are born!' (L Prose Fragment 10) But her Romanticism was unstable. 'Pain' is a word which counts in her vocabulary, it is not to be dismissed as an appearance. She cannot make the essential commitment to the here and now for she often feels that the here and now has to be given up as the price of entering the real heaven. Sometimes she associates heaven with the place 'where dreams are born', the Canaan which was denied to Moses; sometimes she associates it with the very order which did the denying. She does not reconcile her aspiration with her sense of affronted justice. 'On subjects of which we know nothing . . . we both believe, and disbelieve a hundred times an Hour, which keeps Believing nimble.' (L 750) Once again we encounter her mistrust of stable states, as if stability falsified or as if it excluded something. 'The Risks of Immortality are perhaps its charm – A secure Delight suffers in enchantment –'. (L 353)

How she scoffed at or repudiated conventional perspectives! How she valued with characteristic Romantic emphasis the extraordinary, the exceptional, the strange, the grand! 'Contained in this short Life,' she wrote in # 1165, 'Are magical extents', but it is not that poem's thrilled sense of the travelling soul which is its most significant feature but rather the oscillation between the secure and the precarious which the next two lines record: 'The soul returning soft at night / To steal securer thence.' The pattern is repeated in an intriguing and erotic dreamlike poem (# 520) where a thrilling pursuit ceases at 'the Solid Town' and yet the retiring 'Mighty look' tells us that there are places where it is powerful still. The ambiguities of her letter to Sue contrasting moonlight and stolen love with obedience and conformity are a good guide. For all her complaints she did still recommend the books and she did not herself break the law, hate her parents, live a wild life or take to atheism. Her poetry is set in the moment of taking leave or letting go, it is not placed after the severance of all connection; and there always has to be something to leave. Like Thoreau she went into the wilderness – but not too far.

*Solid* town, *real* life, 'The Heaven God bestow' (# 636): how dull, stale, oppressive. We may recall the stultifying security of those 'Safe in their Alabaster Chambers', or the great, oppressive weight which is effectively imposed by the motionlessness of the (unmentioned) air in 'There's a certain slant of light' which the merest suggestion of a breeze in that poem would remove. However, it is the *strangeness* of the light in that piece which threatens; it is not permanent enough to become familiar, so it threatens as much by going as by coming (like the chuckling wind of 'An awful Tempest'). If (# 1434) 'In insecurity to lie / Is Joy's insuring quality,' might not a final heaven be merely 'The *Good* Man's – "Dividend" –' (# 234 and see # 1357)?

The staleness of permanence is obviously not something to be feared from a temporary heaven on earth. Of Paradise she proclaimed with misleading firmness, 'I have never believed the latter to be a superhuman site. Eden, always eligible, is peculiarly so this noon.' She added the joke, 'While the Clergyman tells Father and Vinnie that "this Corruptible shall put on Incorruption" – it has already done so and they go defrauded.' (L 391) At least once (# 1657) she believed that we daily live in Eden without realizing it and that it was a mistake (# 1684) to think of Eternity as a distant location when it was really an immediate and constant presence. She made heaven personal (Sam Bowles was in it already, 'constantly, instead of ultimately' – L 489), for (# 370):

> Heaven is so far of the Mind
> That were the Mind dissolved –
> The Site – of it – by Architect
> Could not again be proved –

Voltaire thought that if God did not exist we should need to invent him. There is an element of this in Emily Dickinson's sense of heaven (# 1228):

> So much of Heaven has gone from Earth
> That there must be a Heaven
> If only to enclose the Saints
> To Affidavit given.

But we are given the impression that her invention would be different from the official one. The rebelliousness which I have traced in Chapter III flares in 'Earth is Heaven – / Whether Heaven is Heaven or not' (# 1408) and, as for the official one, 'it would affront us / To dwell in such a place –'. At such moments she can show Melville's anger with God (# 1205):

> Of Heaven above the firmest proof
> We fundamental know
> Except for its marauding Hand
> It had been Heaven below.

Yet, upon some such name – Heaven, Paradise, Eden, Canaan – conceivable now, sustainable in future, she built her life.

In part she built it out of falling in love. Out of this she made pieces as various as the quiet wish-fulfilment of being married to a clergyman (# 944) – he meeting some intellectual challenge, she involved with 'some foolisher effect' of sewing or music – the rasping 'Rearrange a "Wife's" affection!' (# 1737) and the cool # 732 where she balances against marriage the lingering sense that domesticity has cost her 'Amplitude, or Awe'. More conspicuously, however, she made out of it the heavenly claims of Romance. 'He asked if I was his'; the world dropped away; 'Eternity it was before/ Eternity was due –' (# 1053). The theme of 'Eternity – obtained – in Time –' (# 800) is recurrent (e.g. # 765) but such poems count not for their insight into love but for the picture they give of her mental world. She makes love a touchstone: everything may be judged against such a depth of experience, she says in the course of what is probably her most developed claim for it (# 1260):

Significance that each has lived
The other to detect
Discovery not God himself
Could now annihilate.

Here, remarkably, was a new perspective on the work of preparation which Increase Mather had allowed to believers: (# 1544) 'Who has not Found the Heaven – below – / Will fail of it above –' for (to Otis Lord) 'Cupid taught Jehovah to many an untutored Mind.' (L 562)

She often referred to other people as 'continents' and her sense of the enormousness of some of them is well given in a remark she made to Sue. The Romantic's sense of the potentiality of an individual becomes, in the reaction of a woman who maintains that she has 'a Finless Mind' and cannot organize, virtually paralysing. 'I must wait a few Days before seeing you –' she writes, 'You are too momentous.' (L 581) We can see why Thomas Higginson said of her: 'I never was with any one who drained my nerve power so much' (L 342b), but this must have been comparable to *her* experience of many people. It is characteristic of her valuation of 'An ablative estate' (# 1741) that what someone else might regard as negative she should prize as a positive in saying that 'To the faithful Absence is condensed presence' (L 587). This chimes with a comment she repeated (L 330, L 788): 'A letter always feels to me like immortality because it is the mind alone without corporeal friend.' The physical, outside world disappeared too quickly, came and went, but the afterglow of 'thought' remained as a – calmer? – consolation of that world.

Given the excitement other people could arouse in her, and the massive claims that she rested on the experience of being in love, the story of a visit from Sam Bowles illustrates the way in which – and with some wit – she subdued her feelings into less volatile thought.

[145]

He had come to see her and she had not appeared, so he had called her down, shouting (probably the word was not 'wretch' but 'damned rascal'): 'Emily, you wretch! No more of this nonsense! I've travelled all the way from Springfield to see you. Come down at once.' She did, was never wittier, and wrote to him afterwards:

> I went to the Room as soon as you left, to confirm your presence – recalling the Psalmist's sonnet to God, [*the quotation ends* 'The love of you'].
>
> It is strange that the most intangible thing is the most adhesive.
>
> Your 'Rascal'.

On the name he had called her she finished with the teasing postscript, 'I washed the Adjective.' (L 515 & n.)

Absences are more 'adhesive', more solid ('condensed'), than bodily presence. Rather than read this sense as the mark of intellectual distinction we should refer the remark back to the destabilizing effort of Puritan thought, to the emphasis of Transcendental idealism – and to nervousness. It comments on the way bodies are experienced. So do two unremarkable poems: (# 1383) the witch's spell is not taken off when the witch goes, nor are the years extinct like dead embers; (# 1115) the bees have gone but their murmuring is in the mind as both a memory of the past and an expectation for next year, and so it is for 'separating Friends', for thoughts about them, 'More intimate with us become / Than Persons, that we know.' (It is easy to see, as an available extension of this theme, the idea that the ultimate absence, death, is thereby a fixative for the ultimate presence – a completion. It is also easy to see immortality as the most 'condensed', most 'adhesive', most real presence.)

Visitors may disrupt settled patterns. When their visits are surprises there is some loss of control (even if only the control of expectation) and a world whose patterns were completely fathomed would be one free of such surprises. History, understood, encourages prediction, which is a measure of control, so Emily Dickinson's treasuring of surprises as surprises is a further sign of her a-historicism and of her potential for awe. (The word 'predictable' tends to take away wonder.)

The greatest visitor of all is life which will never come again (# 1741) but its being 'an ablative estate' (the grammatical case expresses removal) is what fills it with surprise and awe. Her emotional and poetic practice is to love the thrill of the imminent and to linger in a departure because in such moments, related to the firm or solid state but not confined to it, she seemed to have the most secure real, least prone to doubt. (The visitor might not come but that would not remove the anticipation, and the visitor's going would not remove the effect.)

'The Mushroom is the Elf of Plants' (despite its being a fungus) because it is a surprise and because it is ephemeral, but, although she called it nature's 'Apostate', it is an extreme example of a type in this (for example, of the flowers on the care of which she spent much of her time but which in her poems are repeatedly threatened by frost). The mushroom is an overnight traveller, so abrupt an arrival that it seems to be making alibis for itself by being in two places at once – here but gone, gone but here, like a bubble. It does not – slowly – rot. It is appropriate that she should liken the speed of its growth to the presence of a snake which, likewise, is of elusive origins. The mushroom is 'surreptitious'. It stops for but a time as if it were in near-constant motion. It does not belong.

Neither does the snake – so hard to recognize (make familiar) that its presence is established by description

[147]

and not by name, 'A narrow Fellow in the Grass'. It is about its own business, not interacting. Its purposes are so deeply concealed that it moves through its poem as a set of images and not as an identity – 'A spotted shaft', the grass dividing, a habit of cool places, a whiplash that comes alive, a wrinkle. His occasional – visitor's – presence is a set of glimpses and surprises. He, too, is outside a community of everyday expectation, not 'of Nature's People' in their commonplaceness. Emily Dickinson could never have let Emerson accommodate him and make him familiar in the Over-Soul. She always catches her breath, threatened to the marrow.

At some time in her life she made of his wholly unreachable, sliding presence a more explicit, phallic-dream poem (# 1670) in which a worm, initially merely disquieting, is grotesquely tied up with string. The worm becomes, incredibly and unnervingly, a very fine snake, 'ringed with power'. She flatters. He sees through it, recognizing her fear. What follows is a kind of mesmerizing performance without apparent purpose – the snake showing its snakiness:

> Then to a Rhythm *Slim*
> Secreted in his Form
> As Patterns swim
> Projected him.

She flies, towns away. If she had not done so, *he* would have had to leave – though she does not say that in the poem – for if they had become well acquainted she would not have been able to record the thrill of fear as (unconvincing to her and us) a dream. The poem lives on the frisson.

So does 'A route of evanescence' which is about a visit so rapid with characteristics in such a blur that without appropriate identification in a letter it would be incomprehensible – at least as a presentation of a hummingbird. We have to know what we are looking for.

The poem is not looking for anything: it is confronted. The senses are assaulted – that is, they do not identify and anticipate, and they cannot name. This leaves us, once more, with a performance. If there is too much solidity in 'route' and 'wheel' for an occurrence so swift, the rest of the poem is a brilliant grasping at confusion. 'Evanescence', 'resonance', 'rush', are a free, unlocalized release of abstractions, with 'emerald' and 'cochineal' still giving us only clues. But that was it. It has gone: a flurry like sexual disturbance: 'And every Blossom on the Bush / Adjusts its tumbled Head –'. The clothes are straightened – or the feelings are. Even the offered identification from a far-off, Romantic place seems bland: 'The mail from Tunis, probably.' Ah, an *everyday* excitement. The poem settles, claiming merely an impossible, when it has just enacted a mystery: 'An easy Morning's Ride –'.

Against the 'real life' of the communal world and its made history she opposed a realer life which involved beginning from the fact of life at all as a mystery, containing within it the potential of access to 'Enchanted Ground' (# 1118). She never wanted this interpreted in systematic terms, to have it mapped or catalogued, and this is characteristically Romantic. But a system comes out of it nonetheless and it is important not to miss this by, for example, taking her uncritically at her word.

In 1870 Thomas Higginson paid her his first visit and he made sure that he wrote down some of the things she said to him. One of them was: 'I find ecstasy in living – the mere sense of living is joy enough'. (L 342a) It was not the first time she had put on a display for him. However, the display is significant. It is a revealing guide to how she would have liked to be

[149]

taken. Thirteen years later, in a letter sprinkled with sentiments, she said substantially the same thng: 'To have been made alive is so chief a thing, all else inevitably adds. Were it not riddled by partings, it were too divine.' (L 860) But this is not the language of 'After great pain', nor did 'the mere sense of living' produce the complexity of her verse. Why did she simplify? Why did she put on the display?

Generally people more readily claim to be happy than they admit to being miserable. Happiness easily equates with success in life and misery with failure. Happiness implies some measure of control and misery the lack of it. In claiming that 'the mere sense of living is joy enough' Emily Dickinson was claiming to be able to cope, claiming to have balanced the two elements of power and restraint which her poetry in fact shows as dynamic in their uncertainty.

More reliable, I think, is one of the 'Master' letters where she senses the power of feeling as being difficult to manage. She likens herself to the little mother of the big child who can scarcely support him (L 233); and she speaks in a poem about love (# 1286) of the 'Brief struggle for capacity / The power to contain'. All this accords with her feeling the force of energies which do not belong to her – which erupt within her or flood her being from outside – and yet for which she is the vessel: 'For what is each instant but a gun, harmless because "unloaded," but that touched "goes off"?' (L 656) That sense of the volatility of life (like handling unstable high explosive) gives us the characteristic double feeling of her verse, of power *and* incapacity – that she is in the presence of tremendous energy but has no say in its use. No wonder she was fond of absences – which were taming.

The power, mystery and sheer Romantic extraordinariness of life are imaged for her in the volcano.

She had heard, she wrote (# 1705), of volcanoes abroad but any time she wanted to contemplate one she could see 'Vesuvius at Home' (herself). What obviously pleased her was the idea of latent energy. It gave her pleasure to think that the reality was an incalculable ability to remove the world yet this power was so reserved and undemonstrative. Like the life of her perceptions it was unnoticed but more significant than the busy public life in which she took no direct part. Secretive, unassuming, self-reliant, in the poem 'The reticent volcano keeps' the volcano is plainly an example for human behaviour, the type of the strong and silent, tight-lipped potential.

The volcano image gives her the drama of great power revealing itself to shake the lives of the previously complacent with revelations of the real. It is a drama which depends on deceptive appearance, so in # 1146 it is when the volcano is quiet that the city is apprehensive, and not when, in a fine line, 'she shows her Garnet Tooth'. 'Security is loud' in that poem and this is an example of the situation familiar in Emily Dickinson's thought where something is less powerful or significant in accomplishment or realization (as satisfied hunger or poverty relieved by wealth) than in potential. (Though she mistakenly put Etna above Naples the minimal effect of this shows that it is the thought which locks the poem in place.) This loud security suits with 'I fear a Man of frugal Speech' which is likewise in awe in the face of withheld potential.

There is surely something untried and unexamined and less than mature in the self-approval which reassures itself by saying that it could if it would but does not need to? Emily Dickinson writes as if power alone were its own vindication and we need not inquire into its uses. This leaves us with spectacular energy but with dramas which must always finish after the display.

This is an example:

> On my volcano grows the Grass
> A meditative spot –
> An acre for a Bird to choose
> Would be the General thought –
>
> How red the Fire rocks below –
> How insecure the sod
> Did I disclose
> Would populate with awe my solitude (# 1677)

Hers is the terrible power and hers apparently the
ability to contain that power or – an effective under-
statement – to 'disclose' it. Theirs is the misapprehen-
sion, 'the General thought', undifferentiated, for the
rest of the world is merely a notional attendant audience
to 'populate', that is, provide gaping mouths for the
spectacle she could 'awe' them with. However, might
not 'the General thought' provide one or two volcanoes
of its own? But this is not an idea which the poem
admits. The volcano dominates the landscape. Moreover
no question arises of its being just as fair to place
emphasis on the grassy, meditative spot as on the fiery
insecurity whose impressiveness the poem seems to
prefer. Pride in power joins with pride in concealment.

The pattern repeats in 'A still – Volcano – Life'
where the image is applied now not to an individual
but to existence. Its very character is misunderstood
except in obscurer moments, for its quiet is quiet before
the earthquake. In brilliant lines, its 'hissing Corals
part' and cities are enveloped in laval ooze. Is this a
vindication of its power?

It seems to be so. Another poem (# 1419) likens the
setting of the sun to an upheaval of the earth which
might be seismic or more particularly volcanic, 'And
Houses vanished with a roar / And Human Nature hid.'
This produces the valued 'awe', but is it very different

from that spectacular display of divine wrath which emphasized angry righteousness by destroying Sodom and Gomorrah? There is the same sense of an impressive demonstration of the real before which human beings should be properly submissive, as if might manifests the superiority of the sublime over the mundane. 'Cherish power,' Emily Dickinson told Sue (L 583). She appears to have done so herself.

The sense which she had of it as a potentiality requiring containment connects with her feeling that something used is something dissipated or made less interesting by that. Power is really pressure, force working against resistance (# 252): 'Power is only Pain – / Stranded, thro' Discipline.' She does not know what to make of it when the restraint is removed and so we can have a series of conditionals without a positive declaration: 'When . . . if . . . if . . . if . . .' – a set of 'ifs' with no 'then', the subjunctive drive of an imagination which does not wish to be committed:

> I have never seen 'Volcanoes' –
> But, when Travellers tell
> How those old – phlegmatic mountains
> Usually so still –
>
> Bear within – appalling Ordnance,
> Fire, and smoke, and gun,
> Taking Villages for breakfast,
> And appalling Men –
>
> If the stillness is Volcanic
> In the human face
> When upon a pain Titanic
> Features keep their place –
>
> If at length the smouldering anguish
> Will not overcome –
> And the palpitating Vineyard
> In the dust, be thrown?

If some loving Antiquary,
On Resumption Morn,
Will not cry with joy 'Pompeii'!
To the Hills return!

In the word 'phlegmatic' the sophistications of adult-
hood have been applied to one of the whimsies of fairy
tale, for, a moment later, the giant is eating the villages
for breakfast. What else so consumes? War does, with
'appalling Ordnance, / Fire, and smoke, and gun,' 'appalling Men' and leaving 'smouldering anguish'. The con-
vulsions of personal distress are likened to the convul-
sions of volcanic eruption, breaking through surface
composure just as the disruptive discharge utterly de-
stroys the flimsy human organization which has been
erected on the earth's crust. But the wonderful words
which sustain the doubleness of reference do not allow
us past the terms of the parable to say what, humanly,
such disruption would mean, or what humanly would
be the process of restoration. History is monumental,
not alive. We are locked in the figure. Each imagined
extension of the story, each 'if', supplies the security of
a completed analogue for what is an unresolved crisis.
What follows the conjectural failure of containment is
a comparison of the Resurrection of the Dead with the
work of archaeological recovery. It matches the earlier
course of the poem: concealed beneath the surface is
soon-to-be-revealed fire; concealed beneath the surface
is the buried city. There are thus two revelations, and
contained in that juxtaposition is not only the suggestion of compensation of the first by the second but a
suggestion of necessary cost. It is a restatement of the
powerful Christian paradox that losing life is finding
it, but so structured as to suggest that pain might be
rewarded and thus justified. But recovery is from the

outside. It does not take place within the life of the person for it is not within individual control. But the poem is a might-be, its grammar never completed.

The claim on special, Titanic power is the high Romantic claim and it is made starkly in a problematic poem which has been construed and reconstrued over the years:

> More Life – went out – when He went
> Than Ordinary Breath –
> Lit with a finer Phosphor –
> Requiring in the Quench –
>
> A Power of Renowned Cold,
> The Climate of the Grave
> A Temperature just adequate
> So Anthracite, to live –
>
> For some – an Ampler Zero –
> A Frost more needle keen
> Is necessary, to reduce
> The Ethiop within.
>
> Others – extinguish easier –
> A Gnat's minutest Fan
> Sufficient to obliterate
> A Tract of Citizen –
>
> Whose Peat life[2] – amply vivid –
> Ignores the solemn News
> That Popocatapel exists –
> Or Etna's Scarlets, Choose – (# 422)

It is not hard to grasp the poem's basic antithesis of a 'Peat life' which provides dull, sufficient fire and a special 'Volcanic' power which contrasts so markedly with it. More contentious is the way this is used and to decide on that it is necessary to respect the guidance given by the first line where that special power 'went

[155]

out'. The poem distinguishes this special power by referring to it as (brilliant) phosphorus, as (hot) Ethiopia, as 'Popocatapel' and Etna with scarlet lava. By contrast 'Ordinary Breath' is described as steadily burning 'Anthracite' (without flame), as 'A Tract of Citizen' which a gnat's wing could cool to extinction, and as 'Peat' which sees itself as 'amply vivid'. It would take 'A Power of Renowned Cold', 'A Frost more needle keen', than that which terminates 'Ordinary Breath' to 'quench' or 'reduce' the special life. Yet that life *has* been quenched. As 'The Climate of the Grave' gives a temperature 'just adequate' to do the job of extinction 'So Anthracite' is just adequate 'to live'. (Other readings seek to align 'Anthracite' with the phosphor and the volcanic scarlets because anthracite is a special coal. However it is a dull, industrial fuel and the attempted alignment would have the special life 'just' surviving the grave and that ruins the poem's line of thought which begins by accepting that the 'Life' has already gone out. In reading we seem to have to choose between over-compression, as in my account, or that *and* contortion as in some others.) The 'Peat life' will either go on ignoring the 'solemn' fact of volcanic power, or else it will choose Etna's scarlets.

Thus we see the 'Ordinary', the 'Citizen', the visually dull, set against 'a finer', more abundant, visually exciting life – just as, above, we have seen 'the General thought' opposed to the poet's 'fire' and undiscerning 'natures this side Naples' distinguished from 'lips that never lie'. There seems to me no doubt that the poet's preference is for the distinguished and the exceptional against the commonplace life, and we are encouraged to follow her. Was she right?

I think that the choice is a false one, just as the opposition – also recurrent in her work – between private and public is a false one, and it is falsely presented. The more exciting alternative is seen as having command of all the vital energies. It is set not against patient, constructive labour but against a place where the only thing that happens is that grass grows, unchangingly (even the vineyard of 'I have never seen "Volcanoes"' is made to take its character – dust and palpitation – from the volcano). Except in one poem, moreover, it is the volcanic which is allotted the larger consciousness: it knows what they do not. But it is the a-historicity of the choice itself which undermines it.

Emily Dickinson's Romantic model involves an opposition between the volcano and its surroundings (elsewhere – outside her work – the opposition might be the bogus one of 'the individual and society') which makes it virtually impossible to think of 'us', unless the 'us' be no more than a momentary agreement between two conflicting natures and identities, mine and theirs, solitary volcano's and complacent city's.

Her model supposes an individual who has a single nature. The volcano will erupt or not erupt – it will not do anything else. She thinks only of one single identity of purpose and not of someone with a hundred different voices and interests speaking inside her head. In the same way the idea of the volcano and the peat (or the city) supposes that society is single in *its* identity and purpose rather than comprising people who plant asparagus and ladies who have blue rinses (and ladies who have blue rinses who plant asparagus).

It also supposes one set of interests which will be constant (the individual's, the volcano's) and another which will be constant (society's). The image of the volcano and the city cannot account for change, or for uncertainty. It is fixed – in an antithesis of threatened destruction.

Moreover, it puts the individual outside society rather

[157]

than asserting his or her membership, envisaging only one kind of relation between the vast individual and the tiny city, and that obviously an antagonistic one. It does not allow for society as a reciprocity of individual interacting with individual. If we think of Emily Dickinson in volcanic solitude, what is to be said of Maggie Maher, or Thomas Higginson, or Susan Gilbert, or Vinnie? There seems to be room in the landscape for only one volcano. The image is exclusive, and – my main point – it is extraordinarily rigid. It cannot allow that people might be modified by being with other people by slow, perhaps imperceptible, adjustment and accretion. It leaves any question of time – excepting the idea of time exploding – out of account.

There is another volcano poem which has received much attention because it seems to be the poet telling her life and judging it. It seems therefore to be an autobiographical document of the first importance. At any rate it is her most famous claim for individual potentiality. The volcano is a gun:

> My Life had stood – a Loaded Gun –
> In Corners – till a Day
> The Owner passed – identified –
> And carried Me away –
>
> And now We roam in Sovereign Woods –
> And now We hunt the Doe –
> And every time I speak for Him –
> The Mountains straight reply –
>
> And do I smile, such cordial light
> Upon the Valley glow –
> It is as a Vesuvian face
> Had let its pleasure through –
>
> And when at Night – Our good Day done –
> I guard My Master's Head –
> 'Tis better than the Eider-Duck's
> Deep Pillow – to have shared –

To foe of His – I'm deadly foe –
None stir the second time –
On whom I lay a Yellow Eye –
Or an emphatic Thumb –

Though I than He – may longer live
He longer must – than I –
for I have but the power to kill,
Without – the power to die –

The poem tells its story figuratively (the human speaker could not be a gun) and thus seems to offer itself as an allegory requiring an effort of interpretation. To what could it refer? Moreover, it ends with a riddle.

I will begin at the end. Obfuscation is a deliberate part of riddling. The same sound may have different senses; a form of words will be juggled to juggle the mind of the reader, and this happens in the last stanza of Emily Dickinson's poem.

'I than He' becomes 'He . . . than I'; 'may longer' becomes 'longer must'; and 'power to' in the third line is 'power to' in the next (the poet considered and rejected the less riddling 'art to' for line three). The explanatory connection 'for' is very loose since, if we try to read it strictly, we are left with a non sequitur (he must live longer than I do because I do not have the power to die). A gun can kill but cannot die – though how that is to be applied to human life is one of the questions to be resolved in the poem. So the major problem is with the opening two lines of the riddle with each of the poem's two protagonists appearing, impossibly, to outlive the other. In the poet's juggling of meanings 'may' and 'must' offer a means of escape from this intractable situation and thus carry the hermeneutic burden: why *may* I live longer? why *must* he? Does 'may' mean 'it could happen that way', or does it mean 'I am permitted'? Does 'must' mean 'he is compelled to' or does it mean 'I need him to'?

How the poem shifts its ground! 'The Owner' of the first stanza becomes, in a radical change in perspective, 'My Master' in the fourth, and allied with this movement is a change in the other major term, that of the life which is a gun. In the first stanza the gun-life had to be picked out and carried off but thereafter it performs with considerable (collaborative) independence – it roams, hunts, speaks, smiles, guards, and is deadly. 'Speaks', the noise of the gun's discharge, and 'smiles', its flash, keep within the bounds of its mere instrumentality but those bounds are tested by 'I guard' and by the end of the fifth stanza it seems able to do the aiming and the cocking for firing itself. What started as an object has become an eagerly compliant partner and this change is evident rhythmically. The poem's first stanza is checked and controlled in the way that much of Emily Dickinson's verse is ('In Corners' and 'identified' are the major disrupters of a regular flow) but then 'And carried Me away' runs off and, with the second stanza making two great surges ('And now . . . And now . . .), the poem bounds forward in happy gusto. Moreover, why has the free-ranging, unopposed predatoriness of stanzas two and three become so threatened and defensive in four and five? Why by the last stanza have we passed, subdued, from partnership to a question of survival and apparently a wish for death?

The situation of the poem is so volatile because the rapid scene changes occur to satisfy emotional wishes. It is a celebration of perceived power and a confession of incapacity, claiming fulfilment but recording frustration. The life at its centre everywhere seeks notice and endorsement. 'A Loaded Gun – / In Corners', its story is initially of neglected potentiality – 'till a Day' when – as in other Cinderella stories of neglected potentiality –

the life was picked, by chance. The romance of being carried off has been soberly introduced via, as it were, lost property, but after that its joy is unrestrained. The situation celebrated is one of privilege and power expressed in exclusion and killing. The gun-life glories in the noise it makes. The very mountains echo – immediately – and the whole valley reflects back the gun-life's activity. This unobstructed pleasure is continued at night for, though the gun-life is respectably on guard, its thoughts are on the rejected pillow. (It is better to think things than do them, for reasons that I have explored earlier.) Eager to express commitment and doing it through destruction, eager, surely, to receive the approval which such commitment might earn, in the fifth stanza the gun-life so identifies with 'Him' that it seems to share his control of its own approved power. The shaping force in the various managed situations is the emotional need of an imagination that, delighting in its own pictures, rushes into many pleasures, all of a dependent kind – first, uninhibited companionship, then devoted care and gratification, then courageous loyalty in adversity. So the poem is not a history in allegorical form but a daydream which, knowingly, thrills at the power of its own imaginings.

It is saddening – as in those other places where she presents herself as 'daisy' genuflecting before, for example, the (male) mountain (e.g. # 124, # 481, # 106, # 339, L 233, L 248) – to have expression of the energy of life allegedly dependent on male sponsorship as here, but of itself this does not warrant claiming that the masculine pronouns here and elsewhere in her poetry are but splintered parts of her own complex female self.[3] This would be to make a conscript of her and to press her poetry into the service of perceptions which, unfortunately, it will not endorse. What startles

[161]

in the whole corpus of her work is that sentimentality or, as here, wishfulness, consorts with acute knowledge of her own mind – startles because knowledge generally implies control. She recognized control as something outside her – 'I had no Monarch in my life, and cannot rule myself' – and she does so in this poem which, notwithstanding the intervening exuberance, finishes as soberly as it began. As I read it, the riddle is that he has to live longer than she does because *she* needs him to, yet the risk is that she 'may' outlive him. She must have someone in whose life she can subsume her own for, as she admits with open-eyed clarity, she cannot even choose her own death (suicide is not 'death', it is killing).

As with the volcano, so with the gun, the basic thought is of the – sometimes liberating – release of energy. Orthodoxy has always mistrusted such spontaneity (which it identifies as purposelessness). It discouraged the free spirit amongst Quakers and, at the first Pentecost, disciples speaking 'in tongues' were immediately accused of drunkenness (Acts 2:13). 'Divine intoxication' was a metaphor popular with Emily Dickinson, rejoicing solo in a thoroughly Romantic reverie at the dangerous absence of restraint.

> Exultation is the going
> Of an inland soul to sea,
> Past the houses – past the headlands –
> Into deep Eternity –
>
> Bred as we, among the mountains,
> Can the sailor understand
> The divine intoxication
> Of the first league out from land?

Can the sailor understand? No, of course not. He would not be intoxicated if he could. But the poem is not so far gone that it does not keep both sea *and* land in sight. It is not out on the fathomless ocean. It still has its reference-points and this explains not only its coherence as an art-work but also its 'exultation'. It can enjoy leaving because it has something to leave. The headlands and houses are as much part of the seascape as the vineyards, birds, grass and cities are of the volcanic landscape: it needs them.

Something similar is true of the tipsy poem 'I taste a liquor never brewed – / From Tankards scooped in Pearl' (# 214) of which Albert Gelpi amusingly observes that she was writing this '. . . while in the name of orthodox religion her father labored tirelessly for the Temperance League.'[4] 'Debauchee of Dew' she calls herself, but a real one would not be able to get her tongue around the words. It is not a poem whose gaiety will be patient of the gravity of Calvinist divines, nor of the textual attentions of literary critics – neither of whom has a vocabulary suited to jocularity – but it is worth observing that, as with the volcano poems, *she* is the centre of interest. She will drink the more,

> Till Seraphs swing their snowy Hats –
> And Saints – to windows run –
> To see the little Tippler
> Leaning against the – Sun – (# 214)

Such uproarious spectacles, like the unlicensed wit of graffiti-writers, carry little weight – until the Saints or the party-managers get to hear of them. They are part of that Emily Dickinson who chuckled over beating a retreat from a privy, vanquished by a resident spider (# 1167), or who enjoyed the chance for a joke when it offered and so reported one day: 'No one has called so far, but one old lady to look at a house. I directed her to the cemetery to spare expense of moving' (L 285), and on another that her Aunt Elizabeth

was:'"the only male relative on the female side".'
(L 473)

A fly in winter reminds her of spring in the way that a cork reminds a drunkard of his drink ('A Drunkard cannot meet a Cork') and she will delight to be sent that far out of her mind for (elsewhere):

> Did life's penurious length
> Italicize its sweetness,
> The men that daily live
> Would stand so deep in joy
> That it would clog the cogs
> Of that revolving reason
> Whose esoteric belt
> Protects our sanity.

Total knowledge would mean or – elsewhere in her work – be synonymous with death. It is not permitted to see God and live. But she has begun the approach, for she is not identified with 'The men that daily live' – she lives on a different scale than one of day-to-day perspectives and it is notable that such an emphasis on sweetness (set against the linear 'length') threatens movement and sequence (and thereby causality) – sanity is likened to a moving belt. Ecstasy leaves 'deep in joy' and divinely intoxicated, brought to a stop, the 'cogs' clogged, and (# 184) she mocks the ideas of restraining or understanding ecstasy. That would be like drawing 'A Diagram – of Rapture' or putting 'Holy Ghosts in Cages'. Similarly, the merit of something that she has heard (# 503) is that, "Twasn't contained – like other stanza –'.

Power but incapacity, power but restraint, ecstasy but restriction: the paradox for her is that she is (# 1601) 'Immured the whole of Life / Within a magic Prison', perplexed as to 'Why Floods be served to Us – in Bowls' (# 756). Continually allowed glimpses of other dimensions, she is a witness who cannot alter what she sees but who refuses to accept explanations for it because that would be to explain away. The shudder is a shudder, the thrill is a thrill; and steadying, reassuring explanations issuing from the regular, daily world of cause and effect offer only to supplant and cancel them.

Her sunset poems are set at the eclipse of that regular, daily world, characteristically 'Fairer through Fading' in the last flare of the absenting sun. 'Bloom upon the Mountain', 'I'll tell you how the Sun rose', and 'How the old Mountains drip with sunset' are amongst the many poems which represent what might be regarded as the passing away or dissolution of the material world in its familiarity, security and quotidian insularity. They are not merely pretty scenes, therefore, but are at an important juncture in her thought – one which she regards as a test of art. There has been a coming and a going and now absence will be presence condensed, but the poem will not itself *be* the sunset, so each of these comes with the disclaimer: description must fail. Since these are passing experiences the problem for representation is how to be just to exactly that fact of passing away.

In 'How the old Mountains' she uses two main lines of imagery. One is fluid (obvious in 'drip', 'ebbs', 'Billows', but also there in 'hand the Scarlet' and 'full', and in the water bird, 'the Flamingo') and one is fiery (in 'burn', 'Cinder', 'Fire', 'Flambeau', 'glimmer'). Water blazes and fire flows, keeping both spectacular light and the sense of movement.

> How the old Mountains drip with Sunset
> How the Hemlocks burn –
> How the Dun Brake is draped in Cinder
> By the Wizard Sun –
>
> How the old Steeples hand the Scarlet
> Till the Ball is full –
> Have I the lip of the Flamingo
> That I dare to tell?

Then, how the Fire ebbs like Billows –
Touching all the Grass
With a departing – Sapphire – feature –
As a Duchess passed –

How a small Dusk crawls on the Village
Till the Houses blot
And the odd Flambeau, no men carry
Glimmer on the Street –

How it is Night – in Nest and Kennel –
And where was the Wood –
Just a Dome of Abyss is Bowing
Into Solitude –

These are the Visions flitted Guido –
Titian – never told –
Domenichino dropped his pencil –
Paralyzed, with Gold –

The whole scene is secondary: the sunset light is not
observed directly but via reflectors as it colours objects
(until, possibly, 'the odd Flambeau' – though the chief
effect of that is 'on the Street'). This is wizardry and its
secondariness means that the sun, wonderfully present
through its effects, is itself out of the eye. Such consonant chimes and assonantal patterns as '*N*igh*t* –
in – *N*es*t* and Ke*nn*e*l*' and '*T*i*t*ia*n* – *n*ever *t*old' and
internal rhymes ('Brake' with 'draped', 'in' with 'Cin')
keep the ear busy as the 'Visions' which 'flitted Guido'
flit us, too – at the same time that they shine gold on the
last reflector of all in the poem, the open-mouthed artist
Domenichino. We cannot see the houses, we cannot see
the men *not* carrying the flambeau, we cannot see
'where *was* the Wood', we can only hear something –
then, and as an '*A*byss . . . *B*owing'. Domes rise, abysses
fall: neither *can* bow – except out – so there is nothing
for us to see. 'Solitude' is the invisible observer's whose

pencil goes down at nearly the same time as her competitor-artist's, that far sharing his paralysis in the impassably solid stop of 'Gold' which, the chronology of Dusk and Nest and Dome notwithstanding, is the final fact of the afterglow and the transformation of transformations.

In 'Bloom upon the Mountain – stated' the sun is, as in a metaphysical conceit, the seed, and the glowing light which it casts upon the mountain is the 'Bloom' or flower of the opening line and the 'Solemn Petals' of the last but one stanza.

> Bloom upon the Mountain – stated –
> Blameless of a Name –
> Efflorescence of a Sunset –
> Reproduced – the same –
>
> Seed, had I, my Purple Sowing
> Should endow the Day –
> Not a Tropic of a Twilight –
> Show itself away –
>
> Who for tilling – to the Mountain
> Come, and disappear –
> Whose be Her Renown, or fading,
> Witness, is not here –

It is as if someone had come and tilled the mountain and planted the seed whose efflorescence now shows; though, as to whose this blossoming – and fading – might be, there's no witness. As the flower opens, 'expanding' during the course of the poem, the poet contrasts the relationship between that flower (the sunset) and that seed (the sun), which reproduces itself 'the same', with her own claimed lack of such a seed. She 'states', and, while she does, the sun is also making its statement – its non-verbal one, 'Blameless of a Name'. If she had the seed – that is, the quality of the

sun, the skill to reproduce it – then the whole day and
not just the evening would be endowed and we should
have a twilight always and not one that disappeared
past the tropic of night's limit. While the poem has
been continuing, insubstantially, effortlessly, attuned,
the appearance of the mountain has been altering as
the sun drops:

> While I state – the Solemn Petals,
> Far as North – and East,
> Far as South and West – expanding –
> Culminate – in Rest –
>
> And the Mountain to the Evening
> Fit His Countenance –
> Indicating, by no Muscle –
> The Experience –

So we finish with abstractions, relationships ('Fit', 'Indicating', 'Experience') and, as in the previous poem, go
out via a negative ('no Muscle').

'A small Dusk crawls' in 'How the old Mountains'
and something must be there for the 'Dome of Abyss'
to bow to. Here, an unspecified owner of 'Renown'
crosses the page, but it will not do to be heavy-footed
and, from knowledge gained elsewhere in Emily
Dickinson about falling light and images of death
(e.g. # 692), import Old Macabre into these poems.
These are evocations of sunsets and sleights-of-hand
with language. That is their terminus. There is mystery
in the delicately rendered glowing of the light, and
to stamp 'death' on 'The Experience' is to blame it with
a name.

The same is true of the further reach of the imagination which occurs in 'I'll tell you how the Sun rose'.
Bit by bit, 'A Ribbon at a time', she will describe it – so
she confidently says. But, while she affects to be tell-

ing, she is actually showing. The great shining, the great busyness, the great shaking out and loosening and commencement, of a sunny morning is for mimesis not catalogue.

> I'll tell you how the Sun rose –
> A Ribbon at a time –
> The Steeples swam in Amethyst –
> The news, like Squirrels, ran –
> The Hills untied their Bonnets –
> The Bobolinks – begun –
> Then I said softly to myself –
> 'That must have been the Sun'!

Not the 'Ribbon', not the 'Steeples', not the 'Squirrels' or the 'Hills' or the 'Bobolinks' of a churchy country town in birdsong actually *are* the joyfulness of the rising light; but meanings need carriers. The restraint that withdraws, via its own descriptions, from the loud, exuberant confidence of 'I'll tell' to the tentativeness (not now to 'you', but 'softly to myself') of 'that must have been' is a dramatization of a certain type of relation between words and experiences. If we cannot find the word we want we stand disabled socially until someone can, and we communicate clumsily by gestures or, laboriously, by fragments of description. But to do the other thing, to sum up the sunrise, would be to cordon off the event and make it safe. The word then becomes self-regarding: there is no experience that manipulative man cannot 'handle': he can always find some words for it. (Only extreme experiences – of terror, or love, or privation – offer any chance that the seals will be broken for such people.) 'That must have been' puts Emily Dickinson's words at respectful distance. The respectfulness, the awe, is part of the evocation of sunrise.

'The largest fire ever known,' she wrote, 'Occurs each Afternoon.' (# 1114) The aphorism startles, pleases, and leaves the hearer with nowhere to go. Not so the poem. Its second phase offers to begin as if nothing had happened since 'I'll tell you' and sets itself in contrast: 'But how he set – I know not –'. However, since there has been a softening and new sensitivity since the bold start, what this line is now pitched against is itself very gentle. The artful lie of art, confessing incompetence while demonstrating genius, shows in the poem as a properly self-effacing human manner. Where else could we be but in a world of seeming?

> There seemed a purple stile
> That little Yellow boys and girls
> Were climbing all the while –
> Till when they reached the other side,
> A Dominie in Gray –
> Put gently up the evening Bars –
> And led the flock away –

Once again, the risk is of spoiling this by allegorizing it ('The Dominie is God . . .', 'The Dominie is her authoritarian father . . .', 'the Dominie is a factory master . . .'). The Dominie in gray is a dominie in gray. William Blake may help to establish this.

At the close of *A Vision of The Last Judgement* he wrote:

'What,' it will be Question'd, 'When the Sun rises, do you not see a round disk of fire somewhat like a Guinea?' O no, no, I see an Innumerable company of the Heavenly host crying 'Holy, Holy, Holy is the Lord God Almighty.' I question not my Corporeal or Vegetative Eye any more than I would Question a Window concerning a Sight. I look thro' it & not with it.

By his very description, 'a round disk of fire somewhat like a Guinea', he well shows that he lives in the same world as everyone else, the world of serviceable descriptions. Yet he repudiates that world. What do we experience in the sunshine? Do we experience the Newtonian operation of 'a round disk of fire'? Do we not, rather, experience an elation hard to describe – – the world bright in its colours, the sky miles high, warmth on our cheeks? William Blake will describe it: 'an Innumerable company of the Heavenly host crying "Holy, Holy, Holy is the Lord God Almighty."'

We understand things by referring them to other things (even the little-wanted disk is 'like a Guinea'). The important thing, however, is not to *replace* one thing with another, or to suppose that we are in the grip of a single system of meaning which consciousness can do nothing to resist (a system which, however chosen, will usually be referred to by its supporters as 'factual'). It is not the eyeball, any more than it is the window pane, which gives you what you see through it. There is no factual sunset. There is what *we* perceive.

In Emily Dickinson's poem there is purple and yellow in a last energy of light on a stile which may have caught the declining rays just as the street in 'How the old Mountains' caught *those* last rays, or which might, along with the imagined girls and boys, be wholly a created analogue. It is a time of innocence and paradox, unending – as long as it goes on ('climbing all the while'), terminated by the change in light in the waiting grey, the moment of crossover. The high-spirited child-light subsides in the encompassing, gray, schoolmaster-clergyman gravity of the last acts of evening, wholly without coercion, established by use, to the security of the pastor.

Like 'I felt a Funeral, in my Brain' or 'He fumbles at your Soul', like 'No Crowd that has occurred' or 'Because I could not stop for Death', like 'I tie my Hat' or 'It was not Death', the bright poems I have just been discussing are performances. They are obedient to a seemingly fixed pattern presented as a spectacle for commentary. At such performances we are apparently powerless to intervene and, if that confines us, it is also a comfort, a relief, a consolation: there is nothing to be done.

But speechless Domenichino and the poet Emily Dickinson, who disavows knowing or having the ability to tell, are, as I have just been suggesting, not spectators nor merely transmitters but the shapers and enablers of such scenes. No poet, no poem. No poem, no Dominie in gray.

So those able people who believe that this poet stripped words away from experience seem to me to mistake the ways in which words live. As I tried to show at the beginning of this present book, words are a reality. I may say that I do not believe that witches exist, but at Salem 'witch' was a word that cost lives. In those poems of hers that, it has been widely recognized, have the form of definitions she shows that the linguistic life is not a substitute but – well, 'flow' was D. H. Lawrence's word for it – a flow of the current. Out of our experience we make English: English makes us by shaping our experience.

Definitions usually subtract words from the contexts where they operate (and accrete meaning) and make them transportable. This poem shows how hers work in the opposite way:

> Presentiment – is that long Shadow – on the Lawn –
> Indicative that Suns go down –
>
> The Notice to the startled Grass
> That Darkness – is about to pass –

It is not the opening dictionary word which is the find: it is the simple 'startled'. Remove it and the poem becomes bland because 'startled' is the word which makes the poem a dramatic enactment, to *and* fro. What startled the attending grass? Was it the premonitory fact of the shadow, or the explanation for it? We cannot judge, and the inability to register such a complex of feeling till the word ('presentiment') has been found for it is brilliantly recognized here in language's inseparability of public and private.

The great reach of 'presentiment', beyond limit, is given in 'that long Shadow'. Majestically, 'Suns go down' to defeat in a weight of latinate syllable and Anglo-Saxon movement. But this is only one way and a pointer, 'indicative'. Then we are given what never appears in a dictionary, a user using, a transaction. Never mind that it is 'grass' which is the using consciousness, was it a consolation to have that precise 'notice', or did it alarm? It was both. It attached an identity to uncertainty but it confirmed it, too. The double flow of the word 'presentiment' is kept to the end (valuable warning, sorry expectation): massively, darkness will come to pass and, at the same verbal moment, it will pass on.

As this poet, who mistrusted 'stale wisdom' in favour of the living stream (# 1210), whose work did not develop because any idea of learning that she may have had seems to have precluded the idea of developing, whose thought 'clutched' rather than built ('I tried to think'), realized, to catch a moment of insecurity is to stabilize it. Performances are not insecure.

Ceremonies of language shape history. I close with one of her greatest.

'Insect-Sounds?' Thomas Higginson hesitantly pencilled on his copy of 'Further in Summer than the Birds'. From a letter (L 813) we know that he was right. This is a poem about the sound of crickets and the end of summer:

[173]

Further in Summer than the Birds
Pathetic from the Grass
A minor Nation celebrates
Its unobtrusive Mass.

No Ordinance be seen
So gradual the Grace
A pensive Custom it becomes
Enlarging Loneliness.

Antiquest felt at Noon
When August burning low
Arise this spectral Canticle
Repose to typify

Remit as yet no Grace
No Furrow on the Glow
Yet a Druidic Difference
Enhances Nature now

The perceived connection between the two subjects, a sound and an ending, suggests part of the reason for its superiority to the still fine parallel poem, 'As imperceptibly as Grief'. 'Further in Summer' is ghostly. The sound of the crickets haunts summer as the ineluctable fact of its own ending, a requiem, the sound of the season. Of all the noises of the earth none was more elegiac for Emily Dickinson than this invisible one of the crickets (# 1775) and 'As imperceptibly' does not have it. That poem must make its own way through tonal changes of light to its aerial 'escape / Into the Beautiful'. In 'Further in Summer' there is no escape, but instead a temporary lustre and an abiding gravity.

Crickets? Summer? The poem's great reach is into the human character of time with its contrary sensed terminus and unknown infinite extension, and it is a reach achieved by regarding time as a matter of depth, and cycle and ceremony rather than of linear progression – not 'later' but 'further'. 'The Birds' in their migratory pattern give us a measure of precedent so firm in its repetition that everything else can be dated from it and the brevity of reference indicates confirmed, shared knowledge. In relation to summer the birds are fixed, in relation to the birds the crickets are fixed, in relation to life the fixative of time is inescapable – witness this performance to which the poet herself testifies, as impotent as she is in 'I felt a Funeral' but here awed rather than menaced because the movement is not further and further on into hideous uncertainty but to the poise of 'Repose', of which death is but a form and of which this conjunction of constant, hardly noticed, cricket sound and blazing decline of summer is characteristic.

It is the murmurous background noise and not the dominating but temporary burning glow of summer sun which sustains permanent meaning, for, beyond the obvious time-scale of the poem, which is that of passing season (and of passing life), is another of human thought and realization which gives it its final 'now' of marked change when no other change has occurred and which we have to call religious – recognizing that in the poem a Puritan mind has expressed its religious sense by appealing to Catholic Mass and pagan rite. All this – crickets, birds, August sun – has been done before. It is a changeless changing. But 'now' the poet understands the nature of the changing and thus resolves a struggle which has been occurring in the poem's stanzas to place and evaluate. 'Further' promotes and 'pathetic' disparages, 'minor' retards and 'Nation' advances, 'unobtrusive' diminishes and 'Mass' aggrandizes; it is high noon yet August burns 'low', this Canticle 'arise' yet to 'repose' (which is why there is an inversion and that word heads a line): two contrary impulses struggle for ascendancy. They mingle through the delicate attenuation of sound (so persistently heard that it is not consciously heard) which becomes an attenuation of thought, 'A pensive Custom', as if it had passed through a membrane of the mind and become an interior fact.

We are reminded initially of Emily Dickinson's sense that this insect life is portal to another or (# 796, # 1000) her image of the minute gnat and the vast sky, for the poem's opening perspective is one of domination. The crickets, though audible, are minor in a consciousness which at first far exceeds them. But then they merge with thought, imaging it, for their very insignificance on the vastness of the scale – the pathos of their being – is exactly consonant with the poet's own sense of isolation. It is thus a confirmation of her feeling but also, because of the mere existence of such a correlative, an expansion of its otherwise purely personal reference (the double meaning of 'Enlarging Loneliness'). Imperceptibly, this developing harmony between poet and crickets is the beginning of 'Grace'.

When the contradiction between the blaze of life and the decline of death is sensed most acutely in the elegiac cricket noise of high noon, when the inevitable order of ages (most 'antique') seems most unremitting, then out of the very limitlessness of the pathos comes its counter-meaning which changes the antithesis and now makes the 'glow' of summer appear as the contraction of significance in face of the subsuming 'Difference' whose occurrence the poem has enacted. Despite present appearances the 'Glow' will in time be faulted with a 'Furrow' on it changing it, and so the glow cannot be relied on whereas 'Difference' is Druidic, the-cycle-of-centuries old, and the very threatening of the 'Furrow' synonymous with the promise of its Grace.

The great tact with which the poem advances depends partly on the way in which the uninflected verbs, 'be seen', 'arise', 'remit', are not limited by the agency of definite, active subjects. This encourages a passive drift which is at its most ambivalent in 'Remit as yet no Grace' where, without subtraction, the verb allows the poem to bring together its accumulated meanings of referral and sending back and retention. These raw, unshaped verb-forms added to the inversions and compressions mean that there is a threshold of pidgin oddity to be crossed but, in its quiet registry of the great scope of the human facts of pleasure in the power of the summer sun and sadness in the undermining threat of that power's withdrawal and in its delicate absorption of such facts in a moment enlarged by them, I think that this poem is amongst Emily Dickinson's best.

# Notes

## Chapter I: History and Her History

1  Mrs Mabel Loomis Todd in a letter to her parents, quoted Leyda, vol. 2, p. 357.
2  Paul Boyer and Stephen Nissenbaum, *Salem Possessed: The Social Origins of Witchcraft*, Cambridge, Mass. and London, 1974, p. 209.
3  Ronald Reagan, President of the United States of America, in a speech to the National Association of Evangelicals in Orlando, Florida, on 8 March 1983, referred to the Soviet Union as an 'evil empire' and 'the focus of evil in the modern world' (*Guardian,* 9 March 1983, *The Times,* 10 March 1983).
4  R. P. Blackmur, 'Emily Dickinson: Notes on Prejudice and Fact', in *Southern Review* III (Autumn, 1937), pp. 323-47, repr. Blake and Wells, p. 223.
5  Adrienne Rich, 'Vesuvius at Home: The Power of Emily Dickinson', in *Parnassus: Poetry in Review,* 5 (Fall/Winter, 1976) 49–74, repr. Ferlazzo, p. 195.
6  Porter, p. 157.
7  Allen Tate, 'New England Culture and Emily Dickinson', in *Symposium* III (April, 1932) 206–26, repr. Blake and Wells, p. 156.
8  R. P. Blackmur, op. cit., p. 207.
9  Thomas H. Johnson (ed.), *Poems,* vol. I, Foreword, vii.
10  Adrienne Rich, op. cit., p. 182.
11  Mabel Loomis Todd, loc. cit., p. 357.
12  Samuel Bowles writing to the poet's brother, quoted Leyda, vol. 2, p. 76.
13  Sewall, *Life,* vol. I, p. 54.

14 Austin Dickinson, quoted in Millicent Todd Bingham, *Ancestors' Brocades: The Literary Debut of Emily Dickinson,* New York, 1945, p. 167.

## Chapter II: Theatre of the World

1 Gelpi, p. 91.
2 The conventional view of Puritanism is subjected to major challenge in Christopher Hill, *The World Turned Upside Down: radical ideas during the English Revolution,* London, 1972.
3 Perry Miller and Thomas H. Johnson, *The Puritans,* New York, 1938, rev. edn 1963, vol. I, p. 184.
4 Letter from John Dunton, quoted Miller and Johnson, vol. III, p. 414.
5 Increase Mather, *Soul-Saving Gospel Truths,* Boston, Mass., 1703, 2nd. edn 1712, quoted Perry Miller, *Nature's Nation,* Cambridge, Mass., 1967, p. 72.
6 Miller, pp. 76–7.

## Chapter III: Faulting God

1 Sewall, *Life,* vol. II, pp. 476–7.
2 Theodore Parker, 'A Discourse of the Transient and Permanent in Christianity', 1841, repr. Perry Miller (ed.), *The American Transcendentalists: their prose and poetry,* New York, 1957.

## Chapter IV: Nicodemus' Mystery

1 John Searle, 'Beer cans and meat machines', 2nd of the 1984 Reith Lectures, *Listener,* 15 November 1984, p. 16.
2 T. S. Eliot, 'The Metaphysical Poets', in *Selected Essays,* 2nd edn, London, 1934, p. 287.
3 Yvor Winters, 'Emily Dickinson and the Limits of Judgement', in *In Defense of Reason,* Denver, 1938, repr. Blake and Wells, p. 192.
4 John Berger, *Ways of Seeing,* London, 1972, *passim.*

## Chapter V: Of Some Strange Race

1 I follow *Complete Poems* here, as usual, though it seems to me that the variant which reverses the positions of lines 2 and 3 makes easier sense.

2 This is a position which shows in, for example, Robert Weisbuch, *Emily Dickinson's Poetry,* Chicago, 1975, pp. 23–33 and *passim;* Sharon Cameron, *Lyric Time: Dickinson and the Limits of Genre,* Baltimore and London, 1979, pp. 206–8; and most powerfully in Porter, e.g. p. 62.

3 Porter, p. 228.

## Chapter VI: Upon Enchanted Ground

1 T. E. Hulme, 'Romanticism and Classicism' in *Speculations: essays on humanism and the philosophy of art,* London, 1936 edn, p. 118.

2 I follow *Poems* here and give the word 'life'. *Complete Poems* misprints 'lift'.

3 In my view the ablest and most interesting of the discussions of 'My Life had stood a Loaded Gun' (though it will be obvious that I disagree with them) are Adrienne Rich's in Ferlazzo (ed.), pp. 186–8, and Albert Gelpi, 'Emily Dickinson and the Deerslayer: The Dilemma of the Woman Poet in America', *San José Studies,* III, 2 (May 1977), repr. in Sandra M. Gilbert and Susan Gubar (eds.), *Shakespeare's Sisters: Feminist Essays on Woman Poets,* Bloomington, Indiana, 1979, pp. 122–34.

 More generally, Emily Dickinson has attracted continuing interest from feminist critics. Books include: Barbara Antonina Clarke Mossberg, *Emily Dickinson: When a Writer is a Daughter,* Bloomington, Indiana, 1982; Suzanne Juhasz, *The Undiscovered Continent: Emily Dickinson and the Space of the Mind,* Bloomington, Indiana, 1983; Vivian R. Pollak, *Dickinson: The Anxiety of Gender,* Ithaca, NY, and London, 1984. There is forthcoming at the time of writing Helen McNeill, *Emily Dickinson 1830–1886,* 1986. A related work is William H. Shurr, *The Marriage of Emily Dickinson: a study of the fascicles,* Lexington, Kentucky, 1983.

4 Gelpi, p. 134.

# Bibliography

## Poems

*The Manuscript Books of Emily Dickinson,* ed. Ralph William Franklin, 2 vols., Cambridge, Mass. and London, 1981.
*The Poems of Emily Dickinson,* ed. Thomas H. Johnson, 3 vols., Cambridge, Mass., 1955.
*The Complete Poems of Emily Dickinson,* ed. Thomas H. Johnson, 1970.
*A Choice of Emily Dickinson's Verse,* Selected with an introduction by Ted Hughes, London, 1968.

## Letters

*The Letters of Emily Dickinson,* ed. Thomas H. Johnson and Theodora Ward, 3 vols., Cambridge, Mass. and London, 1958.
Sewall, Richard B., *The Lyman Letters: New Light on Emily Dickinson and Her Family*, Amherst, Mass., 1965.

## Bibliographical and Textual

Franklin, R. W., *The Editing of Emily Dickinson: A Reconsideration,* Madison, Milwaukee and London, 1967.
Myerson, Joel, *Emily Dickinson: A Descriptive Bibliography,* Pittsburgh, 1984.
Rosenbaum, S. P. (ed.), *A Concordance to the Poems of Emily Dickinson,* Ithaca, NY, 1964.

## Biographical

Johnson, Thomas H., *Emily Dickinson: An Interpretative Biography,* Cambridge, Mass., 1955.

Leyda, Jay (ed.), *The Years and Hours of Emily Dickinson*, 2 vols., New Haven, Connecticut and London, 1960. A source book.

Sewall, Richard B., *The Life of Emily Dickinson*, 2 vols., New York, 1974; London, 1976.

Whicher, George Frisbie, *This Was a Poet: A Critical Biography of Emily Dickinson*, New York, 1939.

## Historical

Capps, Jack L., *Emily Dickinson's Reading 1836–1886*, Cambridge, Mass., 1966.

Lubbers, Klaus, *Emily Dickinson: The Critical Revolution*, Ann Arbor, Michigan, 1968.

St Armand, Barton Levi, *Emily Dickinson and Her Culture*, Cambridge, 1984.

## Critical

*a) Collections of Essays:*

Blake, Caesar and Wells, Carlton F. (eds.), *The Recognition of Emily Dickinson: Selected Criticism Since 1890*, Ann Arbor, Michigan, 1964.

Ferlazzo, Paul J. (ed.), *Critical Essays on Emily Dickinson*, Boston, Mass., 1984.

MacLeish, Archibald; Bogan, Louise; Wilbur, Richard, *Emily Dickinson: Three Views*, Amherst, Mass., 1960.

Sewall, Richard B. (ed.), *Emily Dickinson: A Collection of Critical Essays*, Englewood Cliffs, NJ, 1963.

*b) By single authors:*

Anderson, Charles R., *Emily Dickinson's Poetry: Stairway of Surprise*, New York, 1960.

Gelpi, Albert J., *Emily Dickinson: The Mind of the Poet*, New York, 1971.

Porter, David, *Dickinson: The Modern Idiom*, Cambridge, Mass. and London, 1981.

Sherwood, William R., *Circumference and Circumstance: Stages in the Mind and Art of Emily Dickinson*, New York, 1968.

# Index

'Abraham to kill him' (# 1317), 75

'The Admirations – and Contempts – of time –' (# 906), 60

'After great pain, a formal feeling comes –' (# 341), 114–16, 126, 180 Chap. V, note 1

'Alone and in a Circumstance' (# 1167), 163

'An altered look about the hills –' (# 140), 86, 90

American Civil War, 12, 31

Amherst, Massachusetts, 11, 24, 25–8, 31, 40

Amherst College, 25, 28

'"Arcturus" is his other name –' (# 70), 81

'As imperceptibly as Grief' (# 1540), 174

'As the Starved Maelstrom laps the Navies' (# 872), 83

'At least – to pray – is left – is left –' (# 502), 72–3

'At leisure is the Soul' (# 618), 96

Auden, W. H., 131

'Away from Home are some and I –' (# 821), 62

'An awful Tempest mashed the air –' (# 198), 143

Beardsley, Aubrey, 124

'Because I could not stop for Death –' (# 712), 51–3, 54, 171

'Because that you are going' (# 1260), 144–5

'Bees are Black, with Gilt Surcingles' (# 1405), 92

'Before I got my eye put out' (# 327), 65–6

'The Beggar at the Door for Fame' (# 1240), 83

Berger, John, 107

'Best Things dwell out of Sight' (# 998), 87

'Better – than Music! For I – who heard it –' (# 503), 164

'Between the form of Life and Life' (# 1101), 104

Bible, 42, 70, 81

'The Bible is an antique Volume –' (# 1545), 42, 43, 81

'A Bird came down the Walk –' (# 328), 71–2

Blackmur, R. P., 16–17, 19

Blake, William, 137, 170–1

'Bloom upon the Mountain – stated' (# 667), 165, 167–8

'The Blunder is in estimate' (# 1684), 143

Boston, 26, 37
Bowles, Samuel, 28, 29, 32, 61, 71, 143, 145–6
Boyer, Paul, 13
'The Brain – is wider than the Sky –' (# 632), 64–5
Brecht, Bertolt, 131
Brontë, Emily, 66
Brown, John, 31
Browning, Elizabeth Barrett, 135
Browning, Robert, 135
'The Bumble Bee's Religion', 79, 81
Bunyan, John, 59

Calvin, John, 17, 34–6, 100
Calvinism, 42, 46–9, 57, 62, 80–1, 91, 98, 103, 135, 138, 140, 163
'A Charm invests a face' (# 421), 83
Church of Calvary, San Francisco, 29
'A Clock stopped –' (# 287), 121–3
'The Clouds their Backs together laid' (# 1172), 53
'A Coffin – is a small Domain' (# 943), 64
'Confirming All who analyze' (# 1268), 89
'Contained in this short Life' (# 1165), 142
'Could mortal lip divine' (# 1409), 92
'Crisis is a Hair' (# 889), 128

'The Daisy follows soft the Sun –' (# 106), 161
'The Days that we can spare' (# 1184), 63
'The Definition of Beauty is' (# 988), 90–1

'Departed – to the Judgement – ' (# 524), 49–50
'Deprived of other Banquet' (# 773), 55
'The Devil – had he fidelity' (# 1479), 43
'A Diamond on the Hand' (# 1108), 83
Dickens, Charles, 85
Dickinson, Austin, 24, 25, 30, 31–2, 39, 61
Dickinson, Edward, 25, 27–8, 31–2, 139–40, 143, 163
Dickinson, Gilbert, 79
Dickinson, Lavinia ('Vinnie'), 31–2, 34, 39, 143, 158
Dickinson, Samuel Fowler, 25
'Did the Harebell lose her girdle' (# 213), 83
'Did life's penurious length' (# 1717), 164
'Did you ever stand in a Cavern's Mouth –' (# 590), 129
Domenichino, 166, 172
Donne, John, 55, 88, 121
'A doubt if it be Us' (# 859), 111
'Drama's Vitallest Expression is the Common Day' (# 741), 99–100
'A Drunkard cannot meet a Cork' (# 1628), 164

'Each Life Converges to some Centre –' (# 680), 103
'The earth has many keys' (# 1775), 174
'Eden is that old-fashioned House' (# 1657), 143
Edwards, Jonathan, 81
Elijah, 105
'Elijah's Wagon knew no thill' (# 1254), 105
Eliot, George, 66

Eliot, T. S., 88, 134

'Elysium is as far as to' (# 1760), 64

Emerson, Ralph Waldo, 17, 34, 99–100, 131, 138–41, 148

Epstein, Jacob, 123

'Essential Oils – are wrung –' (# 675), 109

'Estranged from Beauty – none can be –' (# 1474), 95–6

Evergreens, Amherst, 31, 34

'Exhilaration is the Breeze' (# 1118), 149

'Experience is the Angled Road' (# 910), 102

'Experiment escorts us last –' (# 1770), 89

'Exultation is the going' (# 76), 162–3


'The face I carry with me – last –' (# 336), 60

'The Fact that Earth is Heaven –' (# 1408), 144

'Fairer through Fading, as the Day' (# 938), 165

'"Faithful to the end" Amended' (# 1357), 143

'Far from Love the Heavenly Father' (# 1021), 60

'The fascinating chill that music leaves' (# 1480), 105

'The Fingers of the Light' (# 1000), 176

'The first Day that I was a Life' (# 902), 92

'The first Day's Night had come –' (# 410), 128–9

'Fitter to see Him, I may be' (# 968), 20

'Forever – is composed of Nows' (# 624), 38, 94

'Four Trees – upon a solitary Acre –' (# 742), 68

'The Frost was never seen' (# 1202), 62

'Further in Summer than the Birds' (# 1068), 32, 173–7


Gelpi, Albert, 34, 163

Gilbert, Susan Huntington (Sue), 31–2, 39, 53, 59, 61, 96, 137, 142, 145, 153, 158

'Glass was the Street – in tinsel Peril' (# 1498), 88

'Go not too near a House of Rose –' (# 1434), 143

'God is indeed a jealous God –' (# 1719), 78

'God made a little Gentian' (# 442), 60

'The going from a world we know' (# 1603), 85

Great Awakening, 81

'Growth of Man – like Growth of Nature –' (# 750), 100


'The hallowing of Pain' (# 772), 101

Hardy, Thomas, 50

Harper's Ferry Raid, 31

Harvard University, 25

Hawthorne, Nathaniel, 39

'He fumbles at your Soul' (# 315), 40–1, 171

'He outstripped Time with but a Bout' (# 865), 84

'He was my host – he was my guest' (# 1721), 100

'The Heart has narrow Banks' (# 928), 128

'Heaven is so far of the Mind' (# 370), 143

'"Heavenly Father" – take to thee' (# 1461), 77

[185]

Heller, Joseph, 69
Herbert, George, 46
Higginson, Thomas Wentworth, 29–31, 32, 61, 82, 108, 133–4, 138, 145, 149–50, 158, 173
'The Himmaleh was known to stoop' (# 481), 161
'His Bill is clasped – his Eye forsook –' (# 1102), 102
'His Cheek is his Biographer –' (# 1460), 42
'His little Hearse like Figure' (# 1522), 79, 81
Holland, Dr J. G., 28, 32
Holland, Mrs, 66
The Homestead, Amherst, 25, 27, 31
Hopkins, Gerard Manley, 111
'How happy is the little Stone' (# 1510), 76
'How Human Nature dotes' (# 1417), 83
'How much the present moment means' (# 1380), 62
'How the old Mountains drip with Sunset' (# 291), 165–7, 168, 171
Hulme, T. E., 138

'I am afraid to own a Body –' (# 1090), 46
'I can wade Grief –' (# 252), 153
'I cannot live with You –' (# 640), 111
'I died for Beauty – but was scarce' (# 449), 50–1
'I dreaded that first Robin, so' (# 348), 130, 131–3
'I fear a man of frugal speech' (# 543), 151
'I felt a Funeral, in my Brain' (# 280), 112–16, 126, 171, 175

'I had been hungry, all the Years –' (# 579), 83
'I have never seen 'Volcanoes' –' (# 175), 153–4, 157
'I heard a Fly buzz – when I died –' (# 465), 107, 116–18, 120, 126
'I learned – at least – what Home could be –' (# 944), 144
'I like to see it lap the Miles' (# 585), 26
'I meant to have but modest needs –' (# 476), 73–4
'I measure every Grief I meet' (# 561), 127
'I never hear that one is dead' (# 1323), 93
'I never lost as much but twice' (# 49), 78
'I never saw a Moor –' (# 1052), 26, 88
'I play at Riches – to Appease' (# 801), 42, 83
'I prayed, at first, a little Girl' (# 576), 127
'I saw no Way – The Heavens were stitched –' (# 378), 128
'I shall not murmur if at last' (# 1410), 92
'I should not dare to be so sad' (# 1197), 135–6
'I sometimes drop it, for a Quick –' (# 708), 133–4
'I started Early – Took my Dog –' (# 520), 142
'I stepped from Plank to Plank' (# 875), 92
'I taste a liquor never brewed –' (# 214), 163
'I tend my flowers for thee –' (# 339), 161
'I think to Live – may be a Bliss' (# 646), 94–5

'I thought that nature was enough' (# 1286), 150

'I tie my Hat – I crease my Shawl' (# 443), 96–9, 171

'I tried to think a lonelier Thing' (# 532), 57, 107–8

'I'd rather recollect a setting' (# 1349), 21

'If you were coming in the Fall' (# 511), 87

'If What we could' (# 407), 100

'I'll tell you how the Sun rose' (# 318), 165, 166–71

'I'm Nobody! Who are you?' (# 288), 26, 60

'Immortal is an ample word' (# 1205), 144

'In lands I never saw – they say' (# 124), 161

'In thy long Paradise of Light' (# 1145), 78

'In Winter in my Room' (# 1670), 148

'Is Heaven a Physician?' (# 1270), 80

'It always felt to me – a wrong' (# 597), 82

'It makes no difference abroad –' (# 620), 131

'It might be lonelier' (# 405), 108

'It was not Death, for I stood up' (# 510), 118–20, 171

'It was a quiet seeming Day –' (# 1419), 152–3

'It was a quiet way –' (# 1053), 144

'It would never be Common – more – I said' (# 430), 59–60

'It's easy to invent a Life –' (# 724), 76

'It's such a little thing to weep –' (# 189), 117

'I've known a Heaven, like a Tent' (# 243), 67

Jackson, Helen Hunt, 61

'Joy to have merited the Pain –' (# 788), 125

'The largest Fire ever known' (# 1114), 169

Lawrence, D. H., 91, 172

'Lest any doubt that we are glad that they were born Today' (# 1156), 57

'A Light exists in Spring' (# 812), 20, 90

'Lightly stepped a yellow star' (# 1672), 76

'The Lilac is an ancient Shrub' (# 1241), 88

'A little East of Jordan' (# 59), 84–5

'The Loneliness One dare not sound –' (# 777), 57

'Long Years apart – can make no' (# 1383), 146

Lord, Otis, 29, 145

'A loss of something ever felt I' (# 959), 99

'Love – is anterior to Life –' (# 917), 94

'Love – is that later Thing than Death –' (# 924), 94

MacLeish, Archibald, 23–4

Maher, Maggie, 34, 158

Mather, Reverend Cotton, 12, 13, 45

Mather, Increase, 45, 145

Melville, Herman, 39, 144

Miller, Arthur, 34

Miller, Perry, 45

'More Life – went out – when He went' (# 422), 155–7, 180 Chap. VI, note 2

'The Morning after Woe –' (# 364), 133

Moses, 82, 84, 141

Mount Holyoke Female
    Seminary, 26, 40

'Much madness is divinest
    Sense' (# 435), 66

'The murmuring of Bees, has
    ceased' (# 1115), 146

'The Mushroom is the Elf of
    Plants' (# 1298), 147–8

'My Faith is larger than the
    Hills' (# 766), 94

'My Life had stood – a Loaded
    Gun – ' (# 754), 158–62, 180
    Chap. VI, note 3

'My period had come for
    Prayer – ' (# 564), 73

'My Portion is Defeat – today –'
    (# 639), 83

'My Soul – accused me – And I
    quailed – ' (# 753), 56–7, 58–9

A narrow Fellow in the Grass'
    (# 986), 25–6, 139, 147–8

'"Nature" is what we see'
    (# 668), 89–90

New England, 34

Nicodemus, 86–7, 90

Nissenbaum, Stephen, 13

'No Crowd that has occurred'
    (# 515), 47–9, 171

'No man saw awe, nor to his
    house' (# 1733), 92

Norcross, Frances, 30

Norcross, Louise, 30

'Not probable – The barest
    Chance' (# 346), 74

'Not "Revelation" – 'tis – that
    waits' (# 685), 64

'Obtaining but our own Extent'
    (# 1543), 76–7

'Of Consciousness, her awful
    Mate' (# 894), 56–8, 107

'Of course – I prayed – ' (# 376),
    72

'Of God we ask one favor'
    (# 1601), 77, 164

'Of so divine a Loss' (# 1179), 20

'On a Columnar Self' (# 789), 55,
    56

'On my volcano grows the Grass'
    (# 1677), 152

'One Blessing had I than the
    rest' (# 756), 164

'One Crucifixion is recorded –
    only – ' (# 553), 130–1

'One need not be a Chamber – to
    be Haunted' (# 670), 56, 107

'Only a Shrine, but Mine'
    (# 918), 101

'The Opening and the Close'
    (# 1047), 87, 100

'Our little Kinsmen – after Rain'
    (# 885), 71

'Ourselves we do inter with
    sweet derision' (# 1144),
    79

'The Outer – from the Inner'
    (# 451), 66

'The overtakelessness of those'
    (# 1691), 62

'Pain has an element of Blank – '
    (# 650), 111

'Papa above!' (# 61), 78, 80–1

Parker, Theodore, 75

'Partake as doth the bee' (# 994),
    83

Philadelphia, 26

Pierpont, John, 69

'A Plated Life – diversified'
    (# 806), 20

Platonism, 135

Poe, Edgar Allan, 57

Porter, David, 17, 123

Porter family, 13

'Prayer is the little implement'
(# 437), 72
'Presentiment – is that long
Shadow – on the Lawn –'
(# 764), 172–3
Proctor family, 13
'Publication – is the Auction'
(# 709), 61, 109
Puritanism, 11, 34, 35–9, 43–5,
55, 68, 70–1, 83, 108, 146
Putnam family, 13

Quakers, 46, 103, 162

'The rainbow never tells me'
(# 97), 89
'Rearrange a "Wife's" affection!'
(# 1737), 144
'Renunciation – is a piercing
Virtue –' (# 745), 20
'Reverse cannot befall' (# 395), 55
Rich, Adrienne, 17
'The Riddle we can guess'
(# 1222), 83
'The right to perish might be
thought' (# 1692), 68
'The Robin's my Criterion for
Tune' (# 285), 34–5
Ross, Alan, 128
'A Route of Evanescence'
(# 1463), 148–9

'Safe in their Alabaster
Chambers –' (# 216), 53–5, 61,
81, 142
Salem, 11–13, 45, 105, 172
San Francisco, 29
'Satisfaction – is the Agent'
(# 1036), 21, 83
Scribner's Monthly, 28
Searle, John, 86
'The Sea said "Come" to the
Brook –' (# 1210), 173

Secret Six, 31
'The Service without Hope –'
(# 779), 23
Sewall, Richard, 69
Shakespeare, William, 99–100,
121
'She died at play' (# 75), 43
'She rose to His Requirement –
dropt' (# 732), 144
Sherwood, William, 47
'So I pull my Stockings off'
(# 1201), 80
'So large my Will' (# 1024), 61
'So much of Heaven has gone from
Earth' (# 1228), 102, 143–4
'A solemn thing – it was – I said –'
(# 271), 95, 101
'A Solemn thing within the Soul'
(# 483), 41–2, 95
'Some – Work for Immortality –'
(# 406), 62
'The Soul has Bandaged
moments' (# 512), 121, 124–5
The Soul selects her own Society'
(# 303), 55
'The Spirit lasts – but in what
mode –' (# 1576), 104–5
'Split the Lark – and you'll find
the Music –' (# 861), 102
Springfield Daily Republican, 28
'A still – Volcano – Life –'
(# 601), 152
'Success is counted sweetest'
(# 67), 83
'The Sun kept setting –
setting – still –' (# 692), 168
'Superiority to Fate (# 1081), 22
'Sweet Mountains – Ye tell Me
no lie –' (# 722), 101
'Sweet – safe – Houses' (# 457),
53
'Sweet Skepticism of the Heart –'
(# 1413), 83

Tate, Allen, 17
Taylor, Jeremy, 116
'Tell all the Truth but tell it
    slant – ' (# 1129), 11
'That after Horror, that 'twas *us*'
    (# 286), 121, 123–4, 128
'That it will never come again'
    (# 1741), 145, 147
'Their Height in Heaven
    comforts not – ' (# 696),
    102
'There came a Wind like a
    Bugle' (# 1593), 105
'There is another Loneliness'
    (# 1116), 55–6, 106
'There is a Languor of the Life'
    (# 396), 129
'There's a certain slant of air'
    (# 258), 143
'These are the Nights that
    Beetles love – ' (# 1128), 124,
    125
'They called me to the Window,
    for' (# 628), 67
'This Consciousness that is
    aware' (# 822), 110
'This is my letter to the World'
    (# 441), 106–7
'This is the place they hoped
    before' (# 1264), 87
'This was a Poet – It is That'
    (# 448), 109
Thoreau, Henry David, 142
'Through the strait pass of
    suffering' (# 792), 61
'Through those old Grounds of
    memory' (# 1753), 106
''Tis whiter than an Indian
    Pipe – ' (# 1482), 68
'Title divine – is mine!' (# 1072),
    130
'To be alive – is Power – '
    (# 677), 95

'To die – without the Dying'
    (# 1017), 101
'To fight aloud, is very brave – '
    (# 126), 62
'To interrupt His Yellow Plan'
    (# 591), 76
'To own the Art within the Soul'
    (# 855), 55
'To pile like Thunder to its close'
    (# 1247), 92
'To put this World down, like a
    Bundle' (# 527), 61
'To see the Summer Sky'
    (# 1472), 23, 89
'To tell the Beauty would
    decrease' (# 1700), 89
Todd, Mabel Loomis, 24–5, 27, 31
'A transport one cannot contain'
    (# 184), 78, 164
'The Trees like Tassels – hit –
    and swung – ' (# 606), 90
''Twas like a Maelstrom, with a
    notch' (# 414), 125–7
'Two – were immortal twice – '
    (# 800), 144
'Two Lengths has every Day –'
    (# 1295), 63

'Undue Significance a starving
    man attaches' (# 439), 83
'Until the Desert knows'
    (# 1291), 67
'"Unto Me?" I do not know you – '
    (# 964), 42

'The vastest earthly Day'
    (# 1328), 64
'The Veins of other Flowers'
    (# 811), 91
'Victory comes late – ' (# 690),
    134–5
'The Voice that stands for Floods
    to me' (# 1189), 64

'Volcanoes be in Sicily' (# 1705), 151

Wadsworth, Reverend Charles, 29
Watts, Isaac, 35, 79
'The Way I read a Letter's – this – ' (# 636), 142
'We do not know the time we lose – ' (# 1106), 68
'We dream – it is good we are dreaming – ' (# 531), 68
'We see – Comparatively – ' (# 534), 21, 66
'What I see not, I better see –' (# 939), 94
'What Twigs We held by – ' (# 1086), 62
'When Etna basks and purrs' (# 1146), 151
'When I have seen the sun emerge' (# 888), 61
'When One has given up One's life' (# 853), 68, 101
'When we stand on the tops of Things' (# 242), 43–4
'Who Giants know, with lesser Men' (# 796), 62, 176
'Who goes to dine must take his Feast' (# 1223), 101
'Who has not found the Heaven – below – ' (# 1544), 145

'Who never wanted – maddest Joy' (# 1430), 21
'Who saw no Sunrise cannot say' (# 1018), 88
'Who were "the Father and the Son"'(# 1258), 81
'"Why do I love" You, Sir?' (# 480), 89
'A Wind that rose' (# 1259), 105
'The Winters are so short – ' (# 403), 78–9
Winters, Yvor, 107
'Witchcraft has not a Pedigree' (# 1708), 95
'Witchcraft was hung, in History' (# 1583), 14–15, 24
'Wonder – is not precisely Knowing' (# 1331), 83, 105
'A Word dropped careless on a Page' (# 1261), 108–9
Wordsworth, William, 137
'A World made penniless by that departure' (# 1623), 103
'The worthlessness of Earthly things' (# 1373), 135

'You constituted Time – ' (# 765), 144
'You'll know it – as you know 'tis Noon – ' (# 420), 89
'You're right – "the way *is* narrow" –' (# 234), 143